Second Edition

# GREAT MINDS

## *The Making...*

### A.E Enoch

TATE PUBLISHING
AND ENTERPRISES, LLC

Published by Tate Publishing & Enterprises, LLC
127 E. Trade Center Terrace | Mustang, Oklahoma 73064 USA
1.888.361.9473 | www.tatepublishing.com

Tate Publishing is committed to excellence in the publishing industry. The company reflects the philosophy established by the founders, based on Psalm 68:11,
*"The Lord gave the word and great was the company of those who published it."*

Book design copyright © 2013 by Tate Publishing, LLC. All rights reserved.

Published in the United States of America

ISBN: 978-1-62902-408-0
1. Self-Help/Motivational And Inspirational
2. Religion/Christian Life/Personal Growth
13.09.25

# *Contents*

*Hints & Tips*

1. There is something inside you that you don't yet know. *You don't know yourself*

2. *You can do much more than you are doing now. All you need is a little more effort.*

3. You can't know 'you', if you don't desire to know 'you', and not until you know yourself; you wont achieve what you can do and what you are made to achieve in life. *Desire to know 'yourself'.*

4. Know what you can do and what you are

made for and go for it. *You can do great things and attain lofty heights.*

5.  No obstacle can stop you from reaching where you are set to reach and achieving what you are set to achieve if you know yourself.

6.  Just believe in you, for *YOU ARE GREAT*.

7.  If you know 'you' plus knowing the Almighty God, then you are unstoppable.

*The difference between you and that great man are simply knowledge and confidence; he knew what he could do and he went for it. you don't know what you can do yet; hence you have remained a mediocre. Discover yourself and make the move.*

A.E.ENOCH

# Introduction

**T**hose who have achieved great things; those who have discovered and initiated great innovations that changed the world; those who have reached the apex of their careers did not achieve them overnight. Their achievements were as a result of their uncompromising effort to discover new grounds and explore new possibilities. Had they not taken the bold step to explore new grounds, they would certainly have remained mediocre persons. However, their unyielding drive to explore new possibilities has launched them into the path of greatness.

You were created a great person. However the responsibility to walk on the path of greatness lies wholly on you. You have the responsibility to choose whether to walk on the path of greatness or to live in mediocrity. The effort you put into exploring new grounds and possibilities represents the choice you are making. God has created over six billion unexplored grounds and opportunities for the over six billion people on earth. Your own ground is waiting for you to explore. Nobody is going to do it for you; for we all have our different terrains to explore. You have to discover and fathom yours. The only way for you to discover and grasp your ground is to discover yourself.

**Discover yourself today and receive the grace for greatness.**

A.E.ENOCH

# Foreword

**M**any years ago we were taught in school that science is discovery. And it was true. But there are things that science is yet to discover that a revelation of God has now brought to everyone that believes and receives Him.

Our lives are empowered from the inside (from the inner man) and the key to dominion and victory in life is the discovery of this awesome power within us.

In this book, A. E. Enoch takes you through a journey of self discovery. And his entire exposition is based on the greatest source of truth – The Word of God. He shows that everyone can discover their true potential, can fulfill their ultimate purpose, and can reign in life through Jesus Christ. He makes powerful truths and principles of achievement come alive in your heart such as:

- Don't underestimate yourself – you don't yet know your full potential
- You carry God's creative ability inside you – and all things are possible for you
- You can achieve anything you set your mind to – so keep your focus on your purpose and stay connected to your power source
- Believe in Jesus and believe in yourself – confidence and commitment are the carriers of your creativity and productivity
- You already have the solution to all of life's problems inside you right now – it's your job to search it out and put it to good use for yourself and for your generation.

We have the grace for greatness inside us right now. We can step into greatness by stepping into the reality of our spiritual life. Knowledge is the key to discovery, and discovery is the power for greatness.

I recommend this book to everyone, young or old that has a dream to be greater than their

culture has told them that they can be. If you have always known that you were made for bigger and better things than you see around you, then this book is for you. If you carry a passion for change, but have no idea how to begin, then this book is for you. There is no career path I know that will not benefit from the wisdom that is revealed in the pages of this book – Lawyers, Doctors, Scientists, Businessmen, Politicians, Economists and financial practitioners, and all those who aspire to these and other relevant positions in society can find direction and inspiration in these pages. Even the retired can find new energy for the years ahead from the inspiration that jumps out of the writings of A. E. Enoch in *Great Minds*.

I encourage you to devote your time to carefully consider the vital lessons in this book. Let them guide you and show you the way to become the person you were born to be. Allow yourself grow into greatness from the inside out. Greatness is inside you. Learn how to let it out every day.

-Tobe E. Godson (MSc, MSM)
London, UK

# Who Am I?

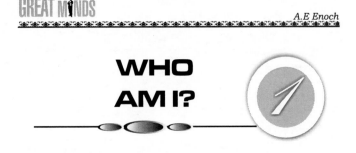

# WHO AM I?

I f you do not appreciate the purpose of any equipment then its abuse is unquestionably inevitable. A purposeless man is bound to abuse his life. We were created with, and for a purpose. God did not create man because he had nothing to do. He created man for a specific reason. *And God said, Let us make man in our image, after our likeness: and let them have dominion... over all the earth, and over every creeping thing that creepeth upon the earth.* Man was craftily and elegantly designed such that he can operate in- line with the purpose for which he was created.

As Man was designed to be God's vehicle for operation on earth, he is therefore an instrument. However, the performance of this human instrument is determined by the user. Just like any other machine invented by man; the operator determines the operation. A computer, for instance, cannot perform more than the user knows about it. An amateur will not do much with the computer, not because the computer can not do much, but because he is a novice and knows little about computer operation. An amateur will therefore operate the computer to the extent he knows and thereby placing a limit on its capacity, whereas a proficient user will fully maximize the computer's potentials. Same applies to humans. The person, to whom you apportion your life, will determine your overall performance in life. If God is the one handling the steering wheel of your life, then you will perform in line with

God's strength and authority; you will exhibit and display all of God's magnanimous qualities and dispositions. But if the devil is the one behind the steering wheel, then the reverse is the case. Your life will surely display the characteristics of the devil. (*Rom 6:16 Know ye not, that to whom ye yield yourselves servants to obey, his servants ye are to whom ye obey*;).For an instrument to effectively operate, it should be handed over to the rightful operator. It should be given to the one who is a master in the use of such instrument. If you therefore want to parade the best of you, the onus is on you to make the first move by handing over your life to your creator who knows everything about your operations and abilities. He is the one that created you, and therefore knows everything about what you can do and what you cannot do. He will never mismanage or abuse you.

Every human being is an instrument of operation. We are all crafted by God to be instruments of change. We all have our specific purposes here on earth; different people have their different purposes, which invariably give rise to our different destinies. Our destiny is a product of our purpose, which is the function of our mindset. This means that a man without a purpose is a man without a destiny; alternatively, a man without a proper mindset is a man with a defective purpose, and ultimately a flawed destiny. To succeed in life you must have a *clearly defined* purpose, and a well set mind to achieve that purpose irrespective of all glitch and odds. God designed each and every one of us for a peculiar purpose and function. Everybody has his own peculiar role to play in the world; individually we function in our own niche, and our collective effort gives the world its continuity. Nobody is born by mistake; and nobody is born to fail. We were all fabricated with the same care and interest, and created to add value to the world; your presence on earth is to add value and flavor to the world. The big question now is "are you adding value to the world or devaluing the world"? Ponder on this.

There *is* however a common and universal purpose for humanity. *And God said, Let us make man in our image, ... **and let them have dominion ... over all the earth**, and over every creeping thing that creepeth upon the earth.Gen 1:26.*

This is the customary purpose of mankind. To rule over the earth. Man is Gods vehicle of dominion on earth and possesses the authority of the almighty God. All men were created to be instrument of dominion on earth. But after the plummet of Adam, this scepter was traded to the devil.

The authority that God gave man lies in man's knowledge of who he is in God. Adam's authority therefore was in his knowledge of himself. When the devil came to Adam and Eve in Eden, his aim was to trade their knowledge of whom they really were with a false knowledge of themselves. That was the only way he could reduce mankind. When he came to Eve; he said in *Gen 3:4-5 (And the serpent said unto the woman, ye shall not surely die: For God doth know that in the day ye eat thereof, then your eyes shall be opened, and ye shall be as gods, knowing good and evil).* The devil promoted a false knowledge of "who man is" to Adam and Eve. The false knowledge was "ye shall be as gods", whereas Adam was already made to be god on earth and not made to be like a god, as declared by the devil! *(Ps 82:6 I have said, Ye are gods )* They got swindled by his scheme, discarded their original knowledge of who they were and consented to him. Little did they

9

know that in their knowledge of who they were was their authority to operate as gods on earth! When they therefore gave up their knowledge for the devil's proposal, they unknowingly gave away their authority to the devil. Hidden inside the devils bid was fear, shame and inferiority complex; all three entered into heart of man the moment he consented. The devil gave Adam fear, shame and inferiority complex in exchange for the authority of God in his life.

*Gen 3:9-10 And the LORD God called unto Adam, and said unto him, where art thou?And he said, I heard thy voice in the garden, and I was* **afraid**, *(FEAR) because I was* **naked**; *(SHAME) and I* **hid myself,** *(INFERIORITY COMPLEX)*. These are the three things the devil used in trading mans authority and dominion from him. He took mans authority and gave man fear, shame and inferiority complex in exchange.    These three things are the mechanism still been use today to limit a man and restrain his progress. What stops a man from possessing his possessions and actualizing his goals today is either fear (he is afraid of the unknown and afraid of failing and therefore cannot take the steps that God might be wanting him to take), shame (he is ashamed of being embarrassed and disgraced and therefore cannot take any bold step), and inferiority complex (he does not believe in himself; have a low self esteem, and sees himself as a "good for nothing"). But the good news is that Christ came to restore the lost authority and dominion to us. *John 10:10 The thief cometh not, but for to steal, and to kill, and to destroy: I am come that they might have life, and that they might have it more abundantly.*

Therefore he that is a believer in Christ has his full authority and dominion restored to him again. He can dominate and exercise God's authority on earth as God originally created for every man to be. But he that has not believed in Christ is still under the devil's influence, and cannot exercise authority and dominion. He is a fallen man and will be limited in all his feats.

Every human being is an instrument. If you give your life to Christ and give him the rule and presiding power over your life, you are handing over this instrument which is your very self directly to God for use. But if you reject Christ authority and rule in your life, then you are directly handing over your very self to the next available option which is the devil. There is no other interpretation to it. It is either you are handed over to God or you are handed over to the devil for use. If you hand yourself over to God to use, then you are having two main purposes on earth.

Your first purpose is God's primary purpose for mankind which is to have dominion and rule on earth.

*And God said, **Let us make man** in our image, after our likeness: **and let them have dominion** over the fish of the sea, and over the fowl of the air, and over the cattle, **and over all the earth**, and over every creeping thing that creepeth upon the earth. Gen 1:26.*

Your secondary purpose is your duty and responsibility to humanity; your services to man and your call. We will first be discussing your primary purpose on earth, which is to have dominion.

## HAVE DOMINION

This concerns everybody, no matter how poor you are or think you are, you are God's instrument of dominion on earth. When God created man, he gave him the scepter of dominion on earth, the devil deceitfully stole this scepter at Eden, but Christ brought it back to us through his death. The authority of the almighty is ours to have if we are in Christ. This is therefore the primary purpose of every child of God: to dominate for God, rule the world, dominate all creatures no matter how big or how fierce, and also exercise authority over evil spirits. Rather, what we see today is the reverse. Men who are supposed to have authority over evil spirits have been terrorized and mesmerized by the same spirits that have been subjected to us. Many are also being terrorized by the same creatures that have been subdued under us. We are creatures of dominion; So long as this earth remains we are made to have authority and rule over the earth with both living and non-living things subjected to us. If you are therefore dominated and oppressed by those things you are to rule over, then you are yet to know who you actually are. Not until you understand and know who you are, your life will continually be tormented by inconsequential elements. Your life will be traumatized with oppressions from evil spirits. Change your mindset today, see yourself as the potentate you have been created to be and re-write your destiny.

In *Ps 82:6-7; I have said, Ye are gods; and all of you are children of the most High. But ye shall die like men, and fall like one of the princes.* Jesus re-echoed this statement in *John 10:34 Jesus answered them, is it not written in your law, I said, Ye are gods?* God has made his children to be gods on earth. We are made to be gods to all things; physical and spiritual, that exists on earth and underneath the earth. If you are a child of God, then you are more than just a man; you are a superior breed of humanity. You are a god on earth. But because you do not realize this and fail to acknowledge who you are, you see yourself living an inferior life, lacking the courage and bravery to live on top. Many people, who claim to know God today, are suffering because of their ignorance of who they are. For your information, ***you are not just an ordinary man, you are a high-breed species; you are a god!*** **If you have received Gods redeeming power and grace in Christ.**

## AUTHORITY OF A GOD

➢ A being with great authority to dominate on earth.

➢ An object of worship.

➤ A ruling force and a spirit that exerts authority.

➤ A super-human being or spirit worshipped as having power over nature, human fortunes, etc.; a deity.

This is who you are when you have Christ. *Ye are gods!* Know this from today that God has made you a god. Therefore live like one. Live with great authority and exercise dominion in your world. You are a super human being! Live like one. No more sickness; no more fear; no more crying; no more poverty; for ye are gods! If you fail to walk in your inheritance and take your position as a god on earth, you will ultimately be trampled upon by the world and by the fallen angels. There is no two way to it. It is either you are dominating or you are being dominated. You can't stand in the middle. You have to either be here or there. If you fail to recognize yourself as a god, the scripture says, then *"you shall die like men and fall like one of the princes"*. What a precondition! God has given you the choice to make; either to live like a god or die like a fallen man.

## PRICE OF IGNORANCE

*Eccl 10:7 I have seen servants upon horses and princes walking as servants upon the earth*

It is like a young prince who inherited enormous wealth from his father; his father also left with him businesses to handle so that he, his children and children after him will have no cause to beg for anything. The dad however did not commit the whole wealth and businesses to his son's hand directly. He conversely stated them in a will for him. Unfortunately this young man does not take interest in anything that is to be read, and as a result, he handled his father's '**will**' with negligence. Consequently, he could not get the fullness of his inheritance because of his indolent approach to his father's will. He was only accessible to the fraction of wealth directly before his eyes, while the rest of his inheritances including the businesses were lost to his father's friends and relatives. This young man being a prodigal child, soon exhausted the few properties accessible to him, and eventually resorted to begging for help and support from his father's relatives and friends. Unknown to him that the same kith and kin have planned to take advantage of his ignorance and live in his inheritance, while he, being the apparent heir was wallowing in penury. The same thing happens to so many people in the world today especially Christians; because they refused to study to know their fathers will for them in the scriptures, they are oppressed far beyond measure. What an insult! Unfortunately this young prince eventually died a beggar while his wealth was lost to strangers. Because this young prince refused to acknowledge and study his fathers written will for him, he ended his life in pain and untold hardship. What a pathetic story for us 'Christians' to learn from.

This is exactly the type of life many people in the world today are living. They have refused to read their heavenly father's will for them (the word of God). And because they do not know what God has freely given to them, they live their daily lives begging from pillar to post; they beg before they eat, beg before they go out, beg for jobs from company to company, beg for clothes to wear, beg for money to spend. Whereas, God owns millions upon millions of companies, billions of cars and mansions. As a matter of fact, God is the owner of everything in the world; all the money in the whole world belongs to him, and he has willed his wealth

freely to his children, so that we will have no cause to whine and be frustrated in our lives. God has prepared the very best for us. But it is so sad to hear that we have refused to acknowledge and accept God's will and provisions for us because of our indolence. This is why many Christians end up like the young prince in our story who had all he will ever need to live a comfortable life on earth, but died in penury because he failed to acknowledge and accept what belongs to him. *Ps 82:6-7.  I have said, Ye are gods; and all of you are children of the most High. But ye shall die like men, and fall like one of the princes.*

Solomon knew this was a prevailing malaise in our world today especially among the children of God and he thus lamented 'saying; *Folly is set in great dignity, and the rich sit in low place. I have seen servants upon horses, and princes walking as servants upon the earth. Eccl 10:6-7;* Knowing who you are begins from <u>knowing why God created man</u> in; G*en 1:26"And God said, Let us make man ... **and let them have dominion**... **over all the earth**..."* and <u>understanding what transpired at Eden</u> between Adam and the devil , *Gen 3:7"And the **eyes** of them both **were opened**, and they knew that they **were naked**;"*

And *in Gen 3:9-11; And the LORD God called..., where art thou? And he said, I heard thy voice in the garden, and I **was afraid**, because I **was naked**; and I hid myself. And he said, who told thee that thou wast naked?* And finally <u>knowing how Christ restored you</u> to where God created you to be which is **"to dominate"**)

*Eph 2:6; And hath raised us up together, and* **_made us sit together in heavenly places_** *in Christ Jesus:*

Note that "heavenly places" here stand for the place of dominion and authority in God, place of dominion and authority over everything on earth and under the earth. You have dominion over the devil, and all his advocates (including sicknesses). Having known God's primary purpose for your life (to dominate on earth for him), you ought to march on to live like god on earth; take the place of dominion and authority on earth and rule your world.

**HERE ARE YOUR DUTIES AS GOD ON EARTH;**

*Ps 82:1-4; God standeth in the congregation of the mighty; he judgeth among the gods. How long will ye judge unjustly, and accept the persons of the wicked? Defend the poor and fatherless: do justice to the afflicted and needy. Deliver the poor and needy: rid them out of the hand of the wicked.*

## We can analyze this verse thus:

1. Be just in your judgment and accept not the person of the wicked, (do not turn away justice for favoritism).

2. Defend the poor and fatherless; be a defender to the poor (both the poor in spirit and the physically poor). Do not ignore them, but rather do your best to uplift them. Give them words of encouragement and assistance in their needs. You are to be exactly like God in heaven *"Isa 41:17; When the poor and needy seek water, and there is none, and their tongue faileth for thirst, I the LORD will hear them, I the God of Israel will not forsake them"*. You are made to represent

God on earth and extend his work on earth. Therefore you ought to give water to the thirsty, give food to the hungry, pray for the sick and heal them, comfort the disheartened, and help the helpless.

3. Do justice to the afflicted and needy; intercede for those with affliction and do not cease to pray for them until they are delivered, liberate those that are possessed; and to those that know not God, give them the word of salvation. (*1 Thess 5:14-15; warn them that are unruly, comfort the feebleminded, support the weak, be patient toward all men. See that none render evil for evil unto any man; but ever follow that which is good, both among yourselves and to all men*). Deliver the poor and needy and rid them out of the hand of the wicked; go forth and liberate those that are under

the bondage of the wicked and set them free (*Matt 10:8; Heal the sick, cleanse the lepers, raise the dead, cast out devils: freely ye have received, freely give.*) God has freely given you the authority to do this; **nothing can resist nor withstand you if you know your rights and authority in God.** The apostles of old knew this and thus they did valiantly for the lord. You too can do the same if you will only recognize the authority given to you. For ye are gods!

The brief therefore of your duties as god on earth is found in *Isa 61:1-3 The Spirit of the Lord GOD is upon me; because the LORD hath anointed me to **preach good tidings** unto the meek; ...to **bind up the brokenhearted**, to **proclaim liberty** to the captives, and the opening of the prison to them that are bound; To **proclaim the acceptable year of the LORD,***

*and the day of vengeance of our God; to* **comfort all that mourn**;..., *to* **give unto them beauty for ashes**, *the oil of joy for mourning, the garment of praise for the spirit of heaviness; that they might be called trees of righteousness, the planting of the LORD, that he might be glorified.* These are your fundamental purposes on earth.

You are a freedom giver! A life giver! A restorer of hope! You, however, will not be able to perform all these duties on earth if you don't understand the will of God for your life. You will, instead, be struggling with how to help yourself, and looking for who will liberate you when you ought to be liberating people.

If you are not exercising dominion on earth; you are still being terrorized by evil spirits, sicknesses and oppressed by the devil in all areas of your life, then you are not fulfilling your fundamental purpose on earth. You may think, oh, it's already too late for me! I have missed so many opportunities.      But know that it is never too late. Now that you have known that you are God's agent of dominion on earth, you are expected to step up to your responsibility and begin to exercise your full authority and adeptness. As you step up to your responsibility, the devil and his activities will automatically give way for you. They will not respect you as a person, but they will bow down and respect God's authority in you. Don't allow the devil to limit you again by those things he contracted with Adam in Eden (fear, shame and inferiority complex- Gen 3:10). Christ has fully restored you to the place of dominion; you are no longer limited; you are unlimited for you are bought with a price (the precious blood of Christ), therefore step up with your authority and go ahead to dominate. You are created to dominate. For ye are gods!

## TIPS

- *The person to whom you handover your life will determine your overall performance in life.*

- *The authority that God gave man lies in man's knowledge of who he is in God.*

- *Not until you understand and know who you are in God, you will continue to live under oppression.*

- *Knowing who you are begins from knowing why God created man.*

*I have said, ye are gods; and all of you are children of the most high   -   Psalm 82:6*

# 2

# What Can I Do?

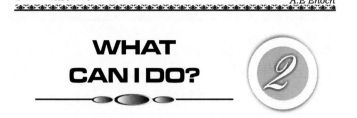

# WHAT CAN I DO?

## WHY AM I HERE?

This is a vital question that most people have failed to ask themselves. When you decline to ask yourself this all important question, you will undoubtedly fail to discover who you really are. The phrase "what can I do" is not mere asking what you can do at a certain place and time' or what you can do as you work in a particular company. It however means knowing what you can do here in this world; what you can do to better humanity and what you can do to impact lives here on earth. What are you going to be remembered for? Don't think "I can't do anything to better the entire mankind, I came from a poor family, I am not educated, or I am being ostracized by my community and family; how then am I supposed to impact lives?" Don't think this way! No matter how poor or deprived you are in your community and family, you can still impact the whole world. Don't feel like all hope is lost. You can do something with your life! You are not yet a write off, because God has not yet given up on you. So long as you where created by God, you are loaded with stuff that can impact the world and make an indelible print. Maybe you are thinking this does not concern me, because my father, or mother or brothers always tell me that I can't do anything good with my life. I am telling you again today that you can do something with your life; you can change the world; you can impact numerous lives.

Gideon was a man from a very poor family in his days and because of his family background, he was seen as an outcast in his society. The pathetic part of the story is that he also saw himself as a complete write off. Now you have to establish the fact that the only person that can write you off in life is yourself. No person can write you off, because your life is not dependent on any man. Your life is dependent only on God. God doesn't reject any body; So God is not going to reject you nor write you off! But you are the only one that can write off yourself. If you have already written off yourself in the past, I want you to rewrite your story today and see yourself in a new light. Put your name back on that list of great men and women that lived.

Gideon is a good example for us to learn from. He saw himself as no body and probably made up his mind that his life was finished and he cannot achieve anything again in life, but to his greatest amazement, the lord sent an angel to him with the great task of delivering Israel from the hand of the Midianite. Can you imagine how stunned Gideon was at the angels salutation to him *"The LORD is with thee, thou mighty man of valour". Judge 6:12* **"A mighty man of valour"**. This was a very weird greeting for somebody that is seen as a societal 'reject'. Notice here that, while Gideon saw himself as a "good for nothing", God saw him as a **"mighty man of valour"**. God is seeing you differently from what you are seeing yourself today. Maybe you are seeing yourself as a failure, but God is seeing you as a success, or perhaps you see yourself that you have nothing to offer the world, God is seeing you as a world changer and as somebody that is to impact thousands of lives. Do yourself a big favor today by beginning to see yourself in a new light. See yourself as God sees you. You will be intrigued to know how God sees you as revealed by Jeremiah, *Jer 29:11 For I know the thoughts that I think toward you, saith the LORD, thoughts of peace, and not of evil, to give you an expected end.* God sees nothing but greatness and everything good in you; this is his thought towards you. Therefore begin to see nothing but greatness and success and everything good in yourself. God is seeing you as a great man. Don't underestimate yourself, the lord sees you as a mighty man of valour, don't see yourself different. See yourself in the same way today; for that is the only way you can truly be who you are created to be.

When Gideon was sent to go and deliver Israel, he brought up a very calculated excuse for why he cannot go.

How can he save Israel his country? How can he save an entire nation? His family is a wretch in a little city in the country.

He is the least in that family, *(judge 6:15 And he said unto him, Oh my Lord, wherewith shall I save Israel? behold, my family is poor in Manasseh, and I am the least in my father's house.)*

What a rational excuse! If he is the least in his very poor family, it means he has nothing! Nothing at all!! But note that God still called him **"a mighty man of valour"** and sent him to go and save Israel as "one man". Whereas Gideon taught he didn't have anything to offer the world, God told him to go and save an entire nation *(Judge 6:16 and thou shalt smite the Midianites as one man)*. This shows that there was something inside Gideon that he didn't know about, but God almighty knew it. If God send you to do something, it means he has seen the potential to successfully carry out that task in you; or else he won't send you. This is to tell us that no body is a complete wretch, so long as you are still alive (*Eccl 9:4 For to him that is joined to all the living there is hope*).Don't look down on yourself, for you can make a change. Don't discard yourself, for you can rise again. Dr. Mike Murdock once said that "all men fall; the great ones get back" up.  Now back to our starting question; **what can I do?**  Before a man can know what he can do, he must first

1.    *Know what he has.*
2.    *Know where he is coming from.*
3.    *Know where he is going.*


Let's critically examine these three headings; so you get a clear picture of what you are created to do.

1.  **Know what you have:** this is the first thing you need to know if you want to discover your purpose. This is the most important aspect of discovering what your secondary purpose on earth is, because if you fail to recognize what you have, then you have indirectly failed to recognize what you can do. And failure to recognize what you can do puts a limit on your performance and it means you do not know who you are. Knowing what you have is the first step to knowing what you can do, and knowing what you can do is the basis of knowing who you are.

2.  **Know where you are coming from**; *Acts 17:28-29   For in him we live, and move, and have our being; as certain also of your own poets have said, For we are also his offspring. Forasmuch then as we are the offspring of God...*

We all have one origin, and our origin is God. We all came from God; there is no two- way to it. God created every body, the good and bad, ugly and beautiful, even the devil was created by him, and to everything God created, he assigned specific purposes; he created the sun to give light in the day; he created the moon to give light at night, he created the plants as source of food for animals and man. The animals also he created to be food to man; but he created man in his image and after his likeness, and the primary purpose of every man is to have dominion over the earth and to cultivate the earth. But our secondary purposes differ.

Now let's start with our primary purposes; the scripture says we are created in the image and likeness of God; we are therefore the offspring of God according to *Acts 17:28 For in him we live, and move, and have our being; as certain also of your own poets have said, For we are also his offspring.* To say a person is an offspring of somebody means he proceeded (came forth) from that person, and carries the biologicalresemblance of that person from which he proceeded in one way or the other. You are an offspring of your father, because you came forth from him, biologically. You have his genes and other characteristics. When the scripture says we are the offspring of God, it is saying we proceeded and came forth from God, and we carry Gods resemblance in our soul and spirit. We are like God; we look like him in image and in likeness. Reflecting on the book of the beginnings, we discover that when God created every other living things except man (the birds, animals, fishes, plants he just called the earth and seas to bring them forth, *Gen 1:11 And God said, Let the earth bring forth grass,*

*the herb yielding seed, and the fruit tree…,Gen 1:20 And God said, Let the waters bring forth abundantly the moving creature that hath life, and fowl that may fly above the earth in the open firmament of heaven…Gen 1:24 And God said, Let the earth bring forth the living creature after his kind, cattle, and creeping thing, and beast of the earth after his kind: and it was so).* But when it was time to create man, God didn't command any other thing to bring forth man, instead he said, "let us make man in our image after our likeness". Every creature has a direct correlation to the source from which God called them. The fishes of the water were called forth from the water, and they return to the water when they die, the animals that were called forth from the earth, have a direct connection with the earth from which they came, and return to the earth when they die. Understand that when we say they return to the source, it means they die and are forgotten; they die and rot either in the sea or on the earth from which they came. But for man God said, "let us make man in our image" meaning God himself is the source from which man came forth and to him shall man return when he dies. Man was formed from the dust of the ground (*And the LORD God formed man of the dust of the ground Gen 2:7*) nevertheless, he was created in the image and likeness of God.

Flesh and spirit, heaven and earth were put together in man. Man was created to glorify the Father, Son and Holy Ghost. Thus he was created differently from all that had been hitherto made. We can therefore construe that for God to choose to bring forth man from himself, whereas he brought forth every other creature from the earth and seas. It means

God must have a special purpose for man. Man must really be a special creature with a special obligation; otherwise he would have been created just like every other creature. You are special to God!

To understand what the scripture means when it says we are created in God's image and likeness; we will look at *Eph 4:24 And that ye put on the new man, which after God is created in righteousness and true holiness,* the new living translation of the Bible says of this same verse; *You must display a new nature because you are a new person, created in God's likeness-righteous, holy, and true.* This infers that we were created after God in righteousness, holiness and truth. And this is interpreted to mean all perfection (power, truth, wisdom, excellence, beauty and all the attributes of God you can think of, because they are all embedded inside God's righteousness and true holiness). We are therefore created to be like God in all his attributes which are power, might, righteousness, wisdom, and excellence.

God's major attribute is that he is a creator, and since we are created in his image, possessing all his attributes; we are also creators (little creators).We are creators in our own scopes and spheres.  That is why *psalm 82:6* says *"I have said, Ye are gods; and all of you are children of the most High"*.  You are created to create, to repair, to build, to invent and innovate, to proffer solutions and be a solution to your world. **That is who you are**. You are a creator in your own scope because of where you came from; you are a progeny of the creator. A Lion can not give birth to a dog; neither can an elephant give birth to a lizard. From a lion comes a lion. The strength and courage are replicated in the cub.

If you allow this knowledge of where you came from to sink into you; then you will for sure know that you can '**do all things**'. You can achieve anything you set your mind on to achieve; you can create anything you desire to create. There is a well of knowledge inside you, there is a river of potentials inside you, and there is an ocean of wealth in you. This was the knowledge that pushed the men of old into building the tower of Babel (their intention was to build the tower to reach heaven; they had that dream because they knew they could do all things. They knew that they were more than just mere physical entity. They knew that they were gods and acted like gods on earth. They were united in mind and in the knowledge of who they were and nothing was impossible to them. God himself acknowledged this and said in *Gen 11:6 And the LORD said, Behold, the people is one, and they have all one language;*

*and this they begin to do: and now nothing will be restrained from them, which they have imagined to do.* If you too will understand that you came forth from God, and possess Gods characteristics; then you will surely know that you can do all things (*Phil 4:13 I can do all things through Christ which strengtheneth me*). The greatest thing that a man can do for himself is to seek to discover his origin, and to know where he came from. That will to a large extent make him to know who he really is. Knowing your source will make you know what you can do. If God is your source, then you can certainly do all things because God can do all things. Jesus gave us a good example to follow because he knew where he came from; he said in, *John 7:29 But I know him: for I am from him, and he hath sent me*. He knew where he came from and displayed the power of the one from whom he came. If only you can acknowledge the fact that you came from God; then you will find yourself living the very life of God and you will operate just like God. And nothing will be impossible to you, just as nothing is impossible with God.

Some people believe they came from apes, and behave like apes in human clothing; that is what they profess and believe. Your life will always go in line with your belief of where you came from. If "what you believe" is that you came from an idol, your life will certainly go in consonance with that idol, and you will be no different from that idol. Filthy and impoverished! But if you believe you came from God and pattern your life after him, then you will be like him in grandeur and in character.

Know where you came from today; for that is the beginning of discovering who you are. You came from God and you have God's name written all over your blood and genes, and this automatically makes you a victor in all your challenges. You have a creative power in you; you have an excellent spirit and a great well of potentials residing in you, which can change the world. The apostles of old turned the world upside down with their gifts because they recognized where they came from and who they belonged to, (*Acts 17:6 ...These that have turned the world upside down are come hither also*).

The four Hebrew children (Shadrach, Meshach, Abed-nego, and Daniel) excelled and did wonders in their time; they were excellent in skills and in knowledge; (*Dan. 1:6-7, Now among these were of the children of Judah, Daniel, Hananiah, Mishael, and Azariah: Unto whom the prince of the eunuchs gave names: for he gave unto Daniel the name of Belteshazzar; and to Hananiah, of Shadrach;*

*and to Mishael, of Meshach; and to Azariah, of Abed-nego... Dan 1:17 As for these four children, God gave them knowledge and skill in all learning and wisdom: and Daniel had understanding in all visions and dreams.)* You too have great potentials and skills because you belong to God. The problem however is that many of us often fail to recognize those abilities that God has deposited in us; we allow distraction and the search for what will not satisfy us to distract us, and we fail to check ourselves for our hidden abilities. You don't belong to this world; you belong to God, you came from him and you are certainly going back to him when you are done here on earth. If you therefore try to reduce yourself to an ordinary man, when you have been made a god, then the real you will fizzle out soon. This is so because when a man tries to be something he is not, he will ultimately loose the essence of who he really is. You are not just a physical entity, you are not just an ordinary man; you are created in Gods image and likeness. You are therefore exactly like God in your spirit. If you therefore try to live like an ordinary man, then you will loose the essence of who you really are as a god to dominate and rule your world. Know that we are not ordinary men, because Christ has restored us back to the original state in which God created Adam before the fall (the state of perfection, power, splendor and purity). Our relationship with Christ is what puts us above the ordinary man who still has the fallen nature in him. Your relationship with Christ has put you above everything physical and natural. You are therefore a problem solver, a solution to the world because you have the spirit of God inside you.

Never you underrate yourself; never look down on yourself and feel inferior about yourself, never envy the rich for your wealth comes from the Lord and its enduring. You are not just a rich folk as they call themselves, but you are blessed. Do you know that there is a big difference between a rich man and a blessed man? A rich man will certainly have money and properties but they are often as a result of human efforts and they may not last; whereas a blessed man lives under divine providence, and never lacks anything. What you have inside you is worth more than all the money in the world. Money can not buy the things God has deposited inside you. If you recognize what you have inside you, you will be amazed to see it bringing great wealth into your hands. But if you fail to recognize what you have, then all you ultimately see is that you are just an ordinary man with nothing to offer. You are not just an ordinary man; you are loaded to solve problems on earth, all you need is the recognition of who you are and where you came from. If you acknowledge this, then you will know that you are exactly like your creator and you are made to be a solution to your world.

Don't you let the devil tie you down with hisinstruments of limitation; you are unlimited in resource and potentialities. His major weapons are fear, shame and inferiority complex. If you can overcome these three satanic weapons of limitation, and you understand where you came from, surely you will rule your world.

3   **Know where you are going:** How can I know if I have arrived, when I don't know where I am going? These where the words of an aged man who lamented over his life when he saw the prosperity of a young chap. The young chap had great vision, courage, and zest to succeed, whereas the old man lived his youthful life in a vacuum.

He could barely distinguish his left from his right when he was young. He had no plan whatsoever for the future. As a matter of fact he didn't know where he was going; and as life will have it, he could not but lament woefully when he was close to the end of the road. He that fails to plan is planning to fail. Knowing where you are going is your sole responsibility to do. Scan voraciously through the pages of your life and identify your talents and your special abilities. Search thoroughly through the core of your heart and identify a vision for your future. Somewhere deep in your heart is a blue print of your future; search it out and run with it. To know where you are going is to know what you are created to do here on earth. God has placed the blue print of our lives and what we are expected to be somewhere in the cores of our heart. But it is our responsibility to search out our future from our heart and run into it with our mind.

Every human being on the face of the earth is here for a purpose, we are all here on assignment from God. However, we should not loose track of the fact that we are going back to God after our sojourn here on earth. We are like passengers in transit and our final goal should be to live forever hereafter. But the question now is: who are you going to live forever with? The life you live here on earth is the determining factor of where you will spend your eternity. Either you live for God here on earth and spend your eternity with him hereafter or you live for the devil here on earth and spend your eternity with him hereafter (*Rom 6:16 Know ye not, that to whom ye yield yourselves servants to obey, his servants ye are to whom ye obey*).

If you therefore know that you are going to be with God, then you will know that your secondary purpose is never to be a thief, a murderer, a prostitute or to be involved in extortion and scam. God hates all these things and those who indulge in them will never get any inch near the divine majesty. (*Gal 5:19-21 Now the works of the flesh are manifest, which are these; Adultery, fornication, uncleanness, lasciviousness, Idolatry, witchcraft, hatred, variance, emulations, wrath, strife, seditions, heresies, Envyings, murders, drunkenness, revellings, and such like: of the which I tell you before, as I have also told you in time past, that they which do such things shall not inherit the kingdom of God*). Your life therefore should be in consonance with Gods life. Living for him everyday should be your priority because you know that you are going to be with him after your transit here on earth. Having known that you are going to be with God after your life here on earth; you should live a life that is becoming of a child of the eternal King; harmonize your life with his divine word. You cannot think of getting wealth by fraud, prostitution, cheating or any other wrong way. God is your source and your provider. If you give yourself to live in God's will, he will not abandon you. He will take you right into your real purpose on earth and he will prosper you in that purpose.

*Ex 14:15-16 And the LORD said unto Moses, Wherefore criest thou unto me? speak unto the children of Israel, that they go forward: But lift thou up thy rod, and stretch out thine hand over the sea, and divide it: and the children of Israel shall go on dry ground through the midst of the sea.* Moses cried unto the lord when the children of Israel where right before the red sea because he did not recognize that the solution to their imminent problem of crossing the red sea was right in his hands . He had the rod of God in his hands (the authority of God) but at this point he did not recognize it, and as a result he didn't know that he already had the solution to his problem. He already had what it takes to overcome all the complications the children of Israel will ever face en route the promise land. God placed his authority in Moses' life in the burning bush, and his rod was made a catalyst for signs and wonders. Moses life changed completely when he met with God in the burning bush; he had divine authority with him and he had an extra ordinary rod in his hand. However, Moses didn't recognize what he had with him; "the divine presence and the miracle rod". He still saw himself as a limited man. That is why when he was before the red sea, he cried to God and did not know what to do whereas the solution was right before his nose. *Ex 14:15-16 And the LORD said unto Moses, Wherefore criest thou unto me? speak unto the children of*

*Israel, that they go forward: But lift thou up thy rod, and stretch out thine hand over the sea, and divide it: and the children of Israel shall go on dry ground through the midst of the sea.*

It's as simple as that! **"Lift thou thy rod and stretch forth thy hand over the sea and divide it"**. God is telling you the same thing today; he is saying "why do you cry" look deep inside you; there is something I have placed in you that will give you solution. You already have the solution to all your problems and the answers to all your questions right inside you; it is left for you to search it out. In the burning bush, God asked Moses, (*Ex 4:2  And the LORD said unto him, What is that in thine hand? And he said a rod.*)But when Moses was before the red sea, God didn't have to ask him again "what is that in your hands" because he had told him what he had' in the burning bush. Instead God rebuked him saying *"wherefore criest thou to me"*.

Now, let's be more personal and realistic; when you met Christ, God deposited something in you. The moment you gave your life to Christ, some talents, energy, gifts and abilities where deposited without reserve inside you.

(*Eph 4:7-8 But unto every one of us is given grace according to the measure of the gift of Christ. Wherefore he saith, When he ascended up on high, he led captivity captive, and gave gifts unto men*).

These gifts and abilities are meant to abide with you through out your life time, and they are to

1.    Help you overcome whatever problem and complexities that come across your way; no matter how enormous that problem

may seem to appear. You are well able to subdue it and over come it, because God has already placed in side you, the energy and ability to overcome all difficulties that come before you. Caleb knew this and he said in (Num 13:30 *And Caleb stilled the people before Moses, and said, Let us go up at once, and possess it; for we are well able to overcome it.*) In verse 31 of that same chapter, the men that went up with Caleb to survey the land of Canaan said *Num 13:31 "But the men that went up with him said, We be not able to go up against the people; for they are stronger than we"*. But because Caleb recognize that God has deposited inside him the ability to overcome all that comes before him; he confessed it and said "we are well able to overcome it". If you fail to recognize God's deposits of abilities and greatness in you, you will keep complaining and seeing impossibility in every situation around you. Everything will look so out of place in your life. All you will keep seeing around you will be the evil report of all situations before you. But if you will just for a moment recognize the strength of God that has been deposited in you then you will soar very high in all your endeavors; there will be no limit to your performance, no mountain you won't climb and there will be no problem you won't overcome. All you need is to know what stuff you are made of; and to harness your inner resources (deposits of great abilities) to achieve your goal.

2.  They will help you get wealth and prosperity in life. God has given abilities to every human being born into this world, to profit with; but those abilities will not

perform in their fullness without God's touch in your life. When God comes into control of your life at salvation, those abilities in you will receive his touch and empowerment, and that's why you become unlimited in your performance. A Christian and an unbeliever who has the same talents will never perform at the same frequency. The child of God will always outshine the unbeliever in performance because he has received a touch of divinity in his talents and has become empowered with Gods own abilities and enablement. He will therefore perform as God himself will perform and will be unlimited in everything, whereas the unbeliever will be limited in performance because he is only depending on his human nature. If you make adequate use of these God's given abilities inside you, you will get everything you want in life. The scripture talks about this in *Prov 18:16 A man's gift maketh room for him, and bringeth him before great men.* This is the essence of God's gifts and abilities in you. They are to make ways for you wherever you go; you cannot be limited because God's ability is never limited. If you are carried into the pit, those abilities will make room for you in the pit. If you are carried to the desert, they will make room for you in the desert. If you are put in a confinement; the abilities are there also to make room for you inside that confinement. Joseph was locked up in prison, and inside the prison his gifts made room for him, and he was taken from prison to be the second in command of the only super power nation in his time. No matter where you go or find yourself, there is always an opportunity for you to excel, there is always a way for you to make wealth and be great, there is always a place for you at the top. This is why those that know God should never complain at all, because they are rest assured that no matter where they find themselves, they will do great things and perform excellently. The scripture said this in *Dan 11:32 but the people that do know their God shall be strong, and do exploits.* By this the scripture is not talking about "know God as your God nonchalantly" as many people will infer. It is talking about those who know God as the unlimited God and recognize Gods gifts and potentials in them with seriousness. These are the once the scripture is referring to when it says "they will be strong and will do exploits". There is no child of God without divine ability and empowerment; God is not a partial God. When you come to him, he freely gives you abilities and empowers you to be effective with the abilities so that you will not lack anything (*Ps 34:10 The young lions do lack, and suffer hunger: but they that seek the LORD shall not want any good thing*). However, the problem is always that many Christians will not seek to discover these divine abilities inside them, and as a result they end up wasting their lives and living sub-standard and wretched lives.

Discover yourself, and you will be amazed at what great things you will do, and how great you will turn out to be.

Joseph discovered his abilities at a very tender age, but his brothers failed to understand this, which was why they sold him out. They didn't believe in his talents. They taught Joseph was doing better than them because of their father's prejudice. They didn't know that Joseph was flourishing, not because of favor from man, but because he knew God and recognized Gods abilities inside him. It was God's abilities in Joseph that brought him the favor he had before their father. They were jealous and got so mad at Joseph that they sold him out into slavery thinking by that they will eliminate his dreams. Nobody can kill your dream except you! If they take you from one place to the other because they want to stop your progress and kill your dream, they will end up doing you a big favor because where they are taking you to will be where God will increase 'you'. When Joseph's brother sold him out, they taught nothing good will ever come out of a slave in a foreign land. To them Joseph's chapter was closed, he could never be any body again. But as God will have it, *"A man's gift maketh room for him, and bringeth him before great men Prov 18:16"*. God's gift in Joseph was alive. Therefore, even in slavery and in a dry land Joseph prospered beyond measure; and his gifts again brought him favor before men; this time not before his father, but before Potipher, and he prospered exceedingly as a slave in Potipher's house. The next page of his life was flipped open, and Potipher's wife was infatuated and wanted to defile him. But because this young man knew God, he refused to consent. This landed him again in trouble; Potipher's wife got mad at him and lied against him. Joseph found himself in prison; but though *he was imprisoned, his talent was not imprisoned*; his gift was well alive and will not sit idle. While Joseph was physically incarcerated, and confined within the four walls of the prison; his ability was very active, and was operating beyond the four walls of the prison to bring Joseph to a place of prominence.

While in prison, Joseph interpreted the dreams of the buckler and the baker. According to his interpretation, the chief buckler was restored to his office, while the chief baker was hanged; *Gen 40:8, 21-22 And they said unto him, We have dreamed a dream, and there is no interpreter of it. And Joseph said unto them, Do not interpretations belong to God?... And he restored the chief butler unto his butlership again; and he gave the cup into Pharaoh's hand: But he hanged the chief baker: as Joseph had interpreted to them.* The chief butler forgot about Joseph after he was restored, but because Joseph's gift was very much alive in him; the gift which was connected to God created yet another room for him in that prison. It is the acknowledgement of God's gifts and abilities in you that connects you to the store house of God where you tap unlimited blessings, no matter where you find yourself. God does not just put money into your hands; he uses the abilities and gifts he has put inside you to give you wealth (*Isa 45:3 And I will give thee the treasures of darkness, and hidden riches of secret places, that thou mayest know that I, the LORD, which call thee by thy name, am the God of Israel*).It is your gift that God will use to push you into the treasures in the dark, and lead you to the riches in the secret. If you therefore fail to recognize these God-given abilities in you, then you have indirectly put yourself under limitation. You will become a limited man in all you do and will be restricted in your achievements and effectiveness. Back to our story of the young Joseph; even after the butler forgot about him when he was restored to his work, the gift inside Joseph which was connected to God went on and created another room for him to excel. God had to orchestrate another opportunity for Joseph to come to limelight because Joseph gift was fully alive in him. Pharaoh now had a very terrible dream and there was no one in the land to give him the interpretation, then the butler remembered that there was a young chap locked up in the prison, who had ability to interpret dreams. The butler had no option than to remember Joseph, even though he forgot him before, as he had never in his life met anyone with such ability. When God puts his divine touch on your talent, you will become a sought after. Men will have no option than to call you for the job! Even though they hate you and don't want you to prosper, they will have no option than to call you, because no other person will be able to do the job as you will do it. Their refusal to use your service will mean they will not get the best in the job. That's why the scripture says in    (*Isa 45:3 And I will give thee the treasures of darkness, and hidden riches of secret places, that thou mayest know that I, the LORD, which call thee by thy name...*). Even your enemies and those that are against you will favor you; because they will be doing harm to themselves if they refuse to favor your cause.

Joseph was brought forth from the prison and cleaned up. He stood before pharaoh and declared the interpretation of his dream *Gen 41:15, 39-40 And Pharaoh said unto Joseph, I have dreamed a dream, and there is none that can interpret it: and I have heard say of thee, that thou canst understand a dream to interpret it...And Pharaoh said unto Joseph, Forasmuch as God hath shewed thee all this, there is none so discreet and wise as thou art:*

*Thou shalt be over my house, and according unto thy word shall all my people be ruled: only in the throne will I be greater than thou.* Joseph's interpretation of pharaoh's dream got him to the top. He became the second in command in the entire land of Egypt. His gift eventually made room for him and set him before kings, *"Prov 18:16 A man's gift maketh room for him, and bringeth him before great men"*.

What started like doddle eventually catapulted Joseph to an exalted position and enlisted him as one of the great men of the Bible. His brothers however tried all they could to limit him and put restriction on him from reaching his destiny, but the gift that God has put inside him will not allow him to be delimited! Joseph's gifts took him to places, gave him honor, wealth, and placed him before kings and great men. These happened because Joseph recognized the abilities that God has put inside of him; and he grasped God's word that says "the gift in a man will make room for him". That same word is for you. God has declared that your gift will make room for you and bring you before great men. That word will never fail in your life if you will take time to discover yourself and appreciate your God-given gifts. If you acknowledge those God's given abilities inside you, they will connect you to God's store house of abundance, and they will open doors and opportunities for you to excel and prosper in all your endeavors and will eventually bring you before kings and great men. The history of mankind portrays that all the great men that ever lived in this world made it great through the continuous excavation and exploitation of their God given potentialities. You too can be great! All you need is to discover yourself and operate with your inner aptitude. God is saying you have the power to change your world! But you cannot change your world until you discover who you truly are and operate in your adeptness. You are powerful specie of humanity; with infinite gifts and abilities.

Gideon is a good example to illustrate what we are talking about. *Judge 6:12-17 And the angel of the LORD appeared unto him, and said unto him, The LORD is with thee, thou mighty man of valour. And Gideon said unto him, Oh my Lord, if the LORD be with us, why then is all this befallen us?...*

*And the LORD looked upon him, and said, Go in this thy might, and thou shalt save Israel from the hand of the Midianites: have not I sent thee? And he said unto him, Oh my Lord, wherewith shall I save Israel? behold, my family is poor in Manasseh, and I am the least in my father's house. And the LORD said unto him, Surely, I will be with thee, and thou shalt smite the Midianites as one man.*

This is the story of Gideon; he was sent by God to deliver the Israelites from the oppression of the Midianites. But Gideon did not recognize his capability. However, the lord knew what stuff he has deposited inside Gideon and what Gideon was capable of doing. Gideon complained and grumbled and concluded that he is not capable of saving Israel from the hand of the Midianite, *"Verse. 15; oh my lord where with shall I save Israel"*

Gideon complained because he has not yet discovered who he was. God had to first make him realize who he was in Him, before commissioning him for the task.

Verse 16 says *"And the LORD said unto him, Surely, I will be with thee, and thou shalt smite the Midianites as one man"*. Gideon was first made to recognize the presence of God with him, and that presence was his succor. If you fail to recognize the presence of God with you, then you will not go far in the task ahead of you. ***The realization of who you are in God is your first step into greatness***. A man does not just wake up in to greatness! It does not happen over night!! It is a process that involves series of steps; of which the first step in that ladder is ***to recognize the presence of God with you and to recognize who you are in God***. The two must go together and are inseparable. They are both combined to give you the first step into greatness. You cannot recognize the presence of God with you and fail to recognize who you are in God. Also you cannot recognize who you are in God and not recognize the presence of God with you. As soon as this realization dawned on Gideon his mind-set was changed, and he took up the colossal task of saving Israel from the hand of the Midianites without an iota of doubt and fear, because he had discovered who he was in God. The greatest thing that can ever happen to a man *is to realize that God is with him; and to discover the God-given abilities inside him*. A person that does this has taken the first step into greatness, and nothing will be able to deter him. It is the hand of God in a man's life that distinguishes him from every other person and sets him to an exalted place. It was this discovery that transformed Gideon and empowered him to face the Midianites dauntlessly. *Judge 6:16 And the LORD said unto him, Surely I will be with thee, and thou shalt smite the Midianites as one man.*

The Lord is saying the same thing to you today. He is saying; "surely I will be with thee

79

and you shall overcome in all you face" only be daring. The big question I will put before you now is; do you recognize that God is with you? You don't need to wait to see any physical manifestation of God before you recognize his presence with you. The fact that you have surrendered your life to him without reserve brings his presence to you without reserve and without measure. (*Ex 33:14 And he said, My presence shall go with thee, and I will give thee rest*). Jesus also said in *John 14:23... If a man love me, he will keep my words: and my Father will love him, and we will come unto him, and make our abode with him.*

It is not about whether you feel God or not. As a matter of fact you don't even have to feel him! *It is not about feelings but it is about knowledge*; just know that He has promised you His presence and acknowledge the fact that He is with you because He cannot lie, and that His abilities are resided in you.

The acknowledgement of God's presence and abilities in you is the beginning of your greatness! The only thing left for you is to search out those abilities and put them to work. You are created to change your world and make a difference; and the apparatus needed to do this is right inside you. Unlock it and put it to work. If you can just for a moment search out your talents and put them to work, you will be amazed at how high you will soar within a short time. Moses is another great example for us to study; when God was sending him to go and deliver the Israelites from Egypt, he looked at himself and concluded that he is not capable of delivering the Israelites from the bondage of the Egyptians. He tried to avoid the task by coming up with a lot of excuses.

*(Ex 3:11,13, Ex 4:1, 10  Ex 3:11-4:10*
*And Moses said unto God, Who am I, that I*

*should go unto Pharaoh, and that I should bring forth the children of Israel out of Egypt?...And Moses said unto God, Behold, when I come unto the children of Israel, and shall say unto them, The God of your fathers hath sent me unto you; and they shall say to me, What is his name? what shall I say unto them?...And Moses answered and said, But, behold, they will not believe me, nor hearken unto my voice: for they will say, The LORD hath not appeared unto thee... And Moses said unto the LORD, O my Lord, I am not eloquent, neither heretofore, nor since thou hast spoken unto thy servant: but I am slow of speech, and of a slow tongue.)*

From the above scriptural verse, we can see all the excuses Moses put up, in other to avoid the task that God gave him; all because he felt he does not have what it takes to carry out the task. Moses did not yet know what God has deposited inside him, but the lord knew what was inside Moses; and therefore will not accept any excuse from him. ***God will never accept any excuse from you for failing to do what you can do***. To all Moses' excuses, God's answer was always pointing to the fact that Moses was very much capable of carrying out the task.

Let's take a critical look at Moses' excuses and Gods response. *Ex 3:11-12*

## UNACCEPTABLE EXCUSES

*And Moses said unto God, Who am I, that I should go unto Pharaoh, and that I should bring forth the children of Israel out of Egypt? And he said, certainly I will be with thee*; if you notice here; God did not just say, "I will be with you" but he added the word "**certainly**", which is to say "unfailingly" when the word "certainly" is used in a sentence, it is used as an affirmative answer to a question or command; which is to say "yes by all means". The verse before us therefore means God was telling Moses, "you don't have to fear about how small and insignificant you think you are to go and stand before pharaoh; I will by all means be with you, even if you stumble and make some blunders. My presence with you will make you bigger than pharaoh." God is saying the same thing to you today. He is saying "you don't have to be afraid of taking that step because I will by all means be with you, even if you make mistakes and look confused". That is why the scripture says in *Rom 8:28* "*And we know that all things work together for good to them that love God, to them who are the called according to his purpose*". God's "by all means" presence with you will convert your mistakes and turn them into strength for you to carry on; he also will turn your mistakes to success in disguise. Moses' question *"who am I that I should go to pharaoh"* is indicative of the fact that he had a problem of inferiority complex. And the only way he can easily overcome that problem is to believe and accept the very fact that God is with him. If you are always seeing yourself as being inferior to other people, then you have that same problem of inferiority complex. You need to recognize that God has promised to be with you by all means. Walk in the mentality that God is with you, and the divine presence qualifies you for greatness and superiority. Don't let anybody look down on you; be daring, lift up your eyes and soar on lofty heights. No matter the status of others, even if they have billions of dollars and chains of cars; never see any body as better than you. The God you have inside you takes you above inferiority status, and puts you on a superiority realm.

Although God promised Moses that he will by all means be with him; Moses still did not believe in himself. He came up with a second excuse; *Ex 3:13 And Moses said unto God, Behold, when I come unto the children of Israel, and shall say unto them, The God of your fathers hath sent me unto you; and they shall say to me, What is his name? what shall I say unto them?* Gods reply this time around was 'tell them "I AM THAT I AM" has sent you. God is using this also to tell Moses that; look Moses, since you doubt my promise that I will be with you. Know that I am the entirety of everything in life! I am the beginning and the end of everything. Before the beginning "was I" I began the beginning! And I have no beginning. "I AM WHO I AM" so you don't need to fret nor doubt my word Moses.

Despite God's words of courage, Moses yet came up with another excuse; *Ex 4:1 And Moses answered and said, But, behold, they will not believe me, nor hearken unto my voice.* This time around Moses was trying to speak for the people he has not even met with. God was very patient with Moses, and asked him in response to his complain. What is that in your hand? God was very patient; whereas Moses was not helping issue. His problem was that he did not believe in himself at all and didn't want to risk going. That was why he came up with so many excuses to try to talk God into believing that he was not capable. Nonetheless his excuses were not acceptable to God. Many of us do the same thing time and time again. We give a thousand and one excuses why we cannot succeed and why we cannot do what we are expected to do. Certainly none of your excuses will be accepted. If God gives you ability, he expects you to use it to bless your world, and he will accept no excuse from you as to why you didn't use it. God told Moses to put his rod down and it became a serpent. This was an act of God to

assure Moses that with him all things are possible.

Moses still finding a way of escape from the great task ahead of him came up with a final question, and thought; well this final excuse will make him leave me alone and go get another person. He said to God in *Ex 4:10 And Moses said unto the LORD, O my Lord, I am not eloquent, neither heretofore, nor since thou hast spoken unto thy servant: but I am slow of speech, and of a slow tongue*. Here Moses was saying. "Lord you can see that I am a stutterer; even as you are talking to me now, you see how I am struggling with my words". God patiently replied him with a question, *Who hath made man's mouth? or who maketh the dumb, or deaf... Ex 4:11*. And in verse 12, God said, *Now therefore go, and I will be with thy mouth, and teach thee what thou shalt say.* When Moses

saw that none of his excuse was approved by God, he opened up and said, "send another person".( *Ex 4:13 And he said, O my Lord, send, I pray thee, by the hand of him whom thou wilt send*). But God being a very enduring God will not give up on Moses; he consequently answered Moses, "if that is what you want, don't worry, I will send Aaron along with you, but for you, you cannot escape this, you must go! Aaron will however accompany you". This proves to us that God is ready to give anything just to make us believe in ourselves and have confidence in his presence with us. But you also need to play your part. Discard all excuses, and step up to work. Don't doubt yourself, and don't doubt Gods' presence with you. God will stick to you so long as you give him the full right to steer your life. Acknowledging God's presence with you will no doubt enable you to understand who you are and what you can do, because his presence will reveal yourself to you and unlock your potentialities. But if you fail to accept the fact that God is certainly with you, you will never truly understand your abilities and you will ultimately live like a stranger to yourself. You will continue to beg for what you already have. Understanding the God that is resident in you is the key to a productive life in God.

One of the biggest problems in Africa today is that, there are a lot of resources: natural resources, human resources, and all kind of resources you can think of, but they are all not being harnessed. This is the simple reason why Africa is still underdeveloped today. We are looking at our natural resources and clapping our hands at them, when we should be harnessing them. But because we are not using these available resources in our land, we are loosing them gradually. The same thing happens in our individual lives. A lot of people fail to recognize their God given abilities, and consequently end up living a backward and very unproductive life. Just imagine this; if Moses had eventually refused to hear God and do what God asked him to do, he would have died a wretched shepherd in Jethro's house and nobody would have heard about him. Imagine with all those great potentials locked up inside Moses, he would have been following sheep! Many people today are still 'following sheep', when they ought to be liberating men and recreating their world. If you are in this shoe, you better shake yourself up, and discover that giant inside you.

I encourage you not to throw away that great vision you have of yourself . You are well able to do it and actualize that dream.

No matter how gargantuan it seems to be before your eyes, just acknowledge God's presence with you, day in and day out and he will bring it to pass.

**TIPS**

- *You can do something with your life! You are not yet a write off, because God has not given up on you.*
- *Don't underestimate yourself, the lord sees you as a mighty man of valor, don't see yourself different.*
- *You are created to create, to repair, to innovate, to proffer solutions and be a solution to your world.*
- *You can achieve anything you set your mind to achieve; just believe in yourself.*
- *You already have the solution to all your problems right inside you; it is only left for you to search it out.*

*"but the people that do know their God shall be strong, and do exploits" - Dan 11:32*

# 3

# Get
# Started

# GET STARTED

I n the preceding chapters we have talked about knowing who you are and why you are here; and the benefits you will get when you discover your purpose. But in this chapter, we are going to be more personal and realistic; in order to help you discover yourself and identify what you can do.

The extent, to which you know yourself, is the extent to which you can maneuver. You cannot operate beyond what you know of yourself. You cannot do what you don't know you can do.

## THE PLACE OF KNOWLEDGE:

It is knowledge that makes a man to act the way he acts. The beggar you see on the street today is not a beggar because he was created to be one; he was never destined to be a beggar. Nobody is destined by God to be a beggar. As the only creator, God loves all his children. *(Jer 29:11 For I know the thoughts that I think toward you, saith the LORD, thoughts of peace, and not of evil, to give you an expected end.)*

This is Gods thought towards his children, irrespective of color, race and nationality. The beggar on the street therefore is a beggar not because he cannot do more with his life, but because he has given up on himself. All he knows about himself is that he is a failure and consequently has no option than to resort to begging. And because he understood himself to be a beggar, his character and emotions revolve around beggarly frame of mind and he eventually became a habitual beggar. Now, that beggar can change himself from being a beggar if he chooses to change himself. All he needs to do is to get another understanding of himself; that he can do something better than just begging. If he allows this understanding to illuminate his psyche, his mentality and emotions will begin to revolve around something better than begging, and he will consequently be changed.

Hosea 4:6 says: *My people are destroyed for lack of knowledge:* it is knowledge that empowers and build a man, whereas lack of knowledge strips a man of his insignia, and ultimately destroys him. Proverbs 24:4-5, reveals thus; "*And by knowledge shall the chambers be filled with all precious and pleasant riches. A wise man is strong; yea, a man of knowledge increaseth strength.*" Your knowledge of who you are and what you can do will take you straight to the top of the ladder! Let's see the life of David as a good example. When the people of God where confronted by Goliath the giant. All the strong men of Israel could not stand to face him, because they where deceived by his size. David, though a small boy, stood to challenge the titanic Goliath. He was not deceived by Goliath's size because he knew that though he (David) was small in stature, he had something bigger and greater than Goliath inside him. It was knowledge that made the difference between David and the other men of Israel; David knew what he has on the inside and he knew what his God was capable of doing through him, but the men of Israel had no such knowledge. *1 Sam 17:23 And as he talked with them, behold, there came up the champion, the Philistine of Gath, Goliath by name, out of the armies of* the Philistines, and spake according to the same words: and David heard them. Verse, 26-27; And David spake to the men that stood by him, saying, What shall be done to the man that killeth this Philistine, and taketh away the reproach from Israel? for who is this uncircumcised Philistine, that he should defy the armies of the living God? verse 31-37 And when the words were heard which David spake, they rehearsed them before Saul: and he sent for him. And David said to Saul, Let no man's heart fail because of him; thy servant will go and fight with this Philistine. And Saul said to David, Thou art not able to go against this Philistine to fight with him: for thou art but a youth, and he a man of war from his youth. And David said unto Saul, Thy servant kept his father's sheep, and there came a lion, and a bear, and took a lamb out of the flock: And I went out after him, and smote him, and *delivered it out of his mouth: and when he arose against me, I caught him by his beard, and smote him, and slew him. Thy servant slew both the lion and the bear: and this uncircumcised Philistine shall be as one of them, seeing he hath defied the armies of the living God.... David said moreover, The LORD that delivered me out of the paw of the lion, and out of the paw of the bear, he will deliver me out of the hand of this Philistine. And Saul said unto David, Go, and the LORD be with thee. Verse 45 Then said David to the Philistine, Thou comest to me with a sword, and with a spear, and with a shield: but I come to thee in the name of the LORD of hosts, the God of the armies of Israel, whom thou hast defied. Verse 50; So David prevailed over the Philistine with a sling and with a stone, and smote the Philistine, and slew him;* David was able to kill Goliath because of his knowledge of his adeptness and Gods strength in him. His brothers and the other men would have been able to kill Goliath if only they had that same knowledge of who they are in God. But because they lacked this awareness; God could not work through them to defeat Goliath. **Their level of understanding have already limited them and put them in defeat**. The same thing happens to children of God always. Your many years in the church have nothing to do with this and cannot change anything; it is rather the knowledge you acquire that changes things. It doesn't matter whether you are a pastor or Bishop; all that matters is how much do you know about yourself and God? You can never operate beyond what you know of yourself and what you know of God. No miracle can happen without knowledge. **Your knowledge either limits you or takes you to the top**. David's brothers had sophisticated weapons to fight with; they also had powerful shields and helmets, but they lacked the knowledge of who they were in God, and that little knowledge they lacked was all they needed to give them the victory. David, on the contrary had no sword nor shield nor helmet. He was insignificant and undersized. When he was offered these weapons, he rejected them outright because he was not used to them. But he had just one rare weapon of great price. That is knowledge! David had the knowledge of what God had deposited inside him and what God was capable of doing through him. This knowledge was actually what killed Goliath. The sling and stone was not what David used to kill Goliath as many people think. To the physical man, they were what he used; but in the spirit realm, it was David's knowledge and understanding of God that killed Goliath. **Understanding gives rise to confidence and confidence generates faith, and faith cannot fail because God respects the exercise of**

**faith in him.** *(But without faith it is impossible to please him: for he that cometh to God must believe that he is, and that he is a rewarder of them that diligently seek him. Heb 11:6)*

In the world today, many people believe they cannot make it and be successful in life, because they have no university degree and no certificates. That is a fallacious concept. It is not about the degrees and certificates you have. Degrees of course will most likely hasten your success, but your degree is not a guarantee that you will be successful. It is not a degree that determines your success. God gives success to whomsoever he decides irrespective of whether you have a degree or not. All he needs is for you to have that knowledge of what prodigious things he can do through you. A man with a thousand and one degrees but no knowledge of what he can offer the world will end up rambling in the dark; but a man that has no formal education, but knows what he can offer to humanity will get to the top of the ladder of life, and nothing will deter him. It is knowledge that makes the difference. Don't allow the idea of "I have no degree" to limit your mind. All you need is to know what stuff you are made of, and I assure you that so long as you have Christ in you, you are an epitome of potentialities. The world cannot fathom the extent to what you can do. You have a lot to offer the world. Take some time to learn about you and the abilities that make up "you" and you will be amazed at what you will accomplish. Some of the early Disciples of Christ had no formal education, but they achieved great things for God. They where able to achieve these great things because of the knowledge they had about God. If you are already seeing yourself as a failure because you did not go to school, I want to sound it loud and clear to you that you are not a failure. Don't let anybody mess you around. You are not junk! God sees in you, those things that every body else ignores. He sees greatness in you, because he has deposited the seed of greatness inside you. He is only waiting for you to wake up and discover that seed which he has put inside you. Maybe your case is "no money to start doing something" you don't have to start very big. Start with the little you have. There is nobody with nothing to start with. You may think there is nothing to start with, but if you skim around you properly, you will discover that you have something to start with; you have as little as five loaves and two fishes to feed five thousand people. Don't ever say you have nothing! **"I have nothing to begin with" is the language of a lazy man**. There is something in your hand; open your eyes wide. In *John 6:7-9 Philip* *answered him, Two hundred pennyworth of bread is not sufficient for them, that every one of them may take a little. One of his disciples, Andrew, Simon Peter's brother, saith unto him, There is a lad here, which hath five barley loaves, and two small fishes: but what are they among so many?* Here the Disciples of Christ didn't see any hope in how they could feed a multitude of five thousand. Philip said, even if we have two hundred penny worth of bread, it will still not be sufficient! And they didn't even have the two hundred pennyworth of bread, to start up and feed a segment of the crowd. Andrew probably trying to make jest said jokingly, "a lad here has five loafs and two fishes" And the other disciples quickly interjected, "you must be out of your mind Andrew, what has five loaves and two fishes got to do with feeding this mammoth crowd". That five loaves and two fishes were so insignificant to the disciples that they didn't take cognisance of them; but that was actually what Christ needed to feed the crowd. Wow! God must be an expert in using the insignificant to achieve extra-ordinary results! In the burning bush, Moses complained to God and grumbled saying " they will not hear me" (*Ex 4:1 And Moses answered and said, But, behold, they will not believe me, nor hearken unto my voice:*) to him, he had nothing to show that he is capable of leading the people of God to the promised land. But God softly asked him, what is that in your hand? *(Ex 4:2)*. Moses saw his rod as insignificant as far as the subject of leading the people of God was deliberated; but that which he saw as insignificant was what God needed to perform his first miracle through Moses. Don't ever say that you have no money and nothing to start with. God is specialized in using insignificant things to achieve great results, if we let him do it. Scan deep inside you and look all around you. What do you see? That thing you are seeing as insignificant and inconsequential may be what God is going to use to make you what he has destined for you.

Therefore, you "don't have a degree" and "you don't have money" is no barrier to halt you.

**All you need is**

1.  Knowledge of what you have inside you; you have God, and that God has given you great potentials.
2.  Be inventive and seek to understand how to use what you have.
3.  Clinch to operate a dogged Faith in God and in yourself.
4.  Cultivate the perpetual will to succeed.

Don't ever compare yourself with any other person; and don't use other people's success to measure yourself. You will never discover who you truly are and who you are meant to be if you measure yourself with another person's success. You will never understand what you can do, if you use another person's work to measure your own ability. If you want to know who you are and what you can do; **Feast your eyes on God!** *Heb 12:2 Looking unto Jesus the author and finisher of our faith;* You are living a life of "struggle" today, because you have failed to acknowledge your proficiency in God. God has no failure in his kingdom; everybody in God's kingdom is potentially great, and successful. So long as you have Christ in you, you too belong to that kingdom. God has written your name in gold among the great men of the world. He is only waiting for you to step up into your inheritance. Greatness and success is your inheritance, and you've got to step into it. *1 John 5:4-5 For whatsoever is born of God overcometh the world: and this is the victory that overcometh the world, even our faith.*

## CONVERTING KNOWLEDGE

After gaining knowledge, your next step is to prudently convert your knowledge into a productive venture. If you already know that you can sing or you can dance, or whatever you know you can do. You are therefore obliged to convert that knowledge to work by doing something with it, and doing what you can do irrespective of what seems to be hurdles on your path. Your knowledge alone cannot get the job done. **Knowledge has to be backed with action to succeed.** If you can sing for instance, don't sit down there saying "I know I am called to be a singer, but I am not fully ready to begin my ministry of singing yet". NO! Start using that gift as soon as you discover it because the time is very short. There are two ways with which you can begin doing what you are made to do; you can start doing it right away with what you have or you can begin doing it by developing yourself and perfecting yourself in that gift. You don't have to sit down idle and let your gift waste away! Don't just sit down idle and say, "God is not asking me to start yet". If God is not asking you to start fully yet, does not mean God is not asking you to perfect yourself more in that gift before you fully kick off. Christ did not start his ministry right away, even though he knew who he was. But he never wasted any time of his life in waiting for a suitable time to start. Christ spent a great time preparing and developing himself. One of such occasions of his self development was his fasting for forty days and forty nights, (Matt 4:2). If you are gifted to be a singer or preacher or an actor, or whatever gift you know you have, take some time and learn more about that gift; seek to understand the challenges and successes that are associated with the gift. Learn from people that have operated in it before you; ask about their successes, confrontations and their mistakes. Hear them speak, listen to their songs, read their books, study their works. The fact that you have that flair does not make you the best. Others have also operated in that same knack before you. Therefore learn from the forerunners. You have to polish your gift everyday like gold so as to bring out the beauty and glory in you. When you are persuaded that you are fully prepared, don't waste anytime. Kick off!

Don't say you don't have the means to start. Begin with the little you have. Put it in the hands of God and watch him do his work; you will be amazed at what great result you will get from that thing you think is little. God is specialized in enlarging little things, if we put the little in his care. There are no hurdles before you; don't let the devil deceive you with that. You are a child of God and no obstacle can prevent you; *Isa 54:17 No weapon that is formed against thee shall prosper; and every tongue that shall rise against thee in judgment thou shalt condemn. This is the heritage of the servants of the LORD, and their righteousness is of me, saith the LORD.* Those things you physically see as complications cannot daunt you. You are too big for them to intimidate! They are just platform for you to climb on to the top. Keep moving without acknowledging any obstacle on your way; whether finance or lack of material resources. Don't even let it hassle you because it can't stop you from reaching your goals. All you need to do is begin with that little thing in your hand. No matter how insignificant it looks in your hand, begin with it. Even if it is as little as 5$ or 10 $ or even a dollar, don't be discouraged; you can do something with it! Just ask God to open your eyes to see what you can do with that little thing in your hands. And just as Christ multiplied those five loaves of bread and two small fishes; he will increase the capacity of that little thing you see as insignificant and he will bring forth plenty from it.

A great man thus; is a great man because of his understanding of what he can do with what he has and his ability to convert his knowledge into action and produce results.

**Focus; a key factor in the path of success:** Focus refers to concentration on a clear cut definition. After you've acquired knowledge and have converted your knowledge to action, you need focus to produce results. If you have knowledge and no focus, you will find it difficult to navigate and doubts will set in and grip your heart. A talent must be harnessed and used habitually otherwise it will fizzle out. The only thing that can keep a talent that has been discovered in steady use is focus. A lot of people with great talents have long given up on themselves; not that they don't know their talents, but they just can't maintain focus. Some people give up so easily after they failed once or twice. You failed the first time does not make you a potential failure. You have the seed of success buried deep within you thus making you a potential success. You failed the first or second time only shows that you have not maximized your adeptness, and you need to put in some more effort. The proficiency for success is already in you; the problem however, is for you to salvage it. That is why you don't quit! Winners don't quit! You keep digging till you hit the diamond deep inside you. Great men launch deep; they understand their knack, and concentrate fully on it. Their knowledge is the pivot on which they build their lives. Knowledge has to converge with concentration and single-mindedness to stimulate an action.

Once your knowledge is sparked up with concentration and action, success is inevitably set in motion. If you must succeed, you must use your mind to concentrate. It is one thing to have great faculty and know that you have it; and it is another thing to succeed with the appliance of your endowment. There are millions of people in the world today who understand their endowment and even began to do something with it. In the long run they ended up in liquidation. Guess you will ask how did they fail with all their abilities? **They lacked one thing; and that is focus.** Focus means to follow a course completely without any iota of distraction from within or without. Christ told Martha, in *Luke 10:41-42; Martha, Martha, thou art careful and troubled about many things: But one thing is needful: and Mary hath chosen that good part.* Martha lacked focus! That was her major problem. Mary on the other hand was much focused, and the lord lauded her for it. Many people in spite of their proficiency cannot achieve anything simply because they lack focus. To such, even if you give them the whole money in the world to promote their talents, they will still fail because they lack focus.

*2 Kings 2:9-10 And it came to pass, when they were gone over, that Elijah said unto Elisha, Ask what I shall do for thee, before I be taken away from thee. And Elisha said, I pray thee, let a double portion of thy spirit be upon me. And he said, Thou hast asked a hard thing: nevertheless, if thou see me when I am taken from thee, it shall be so unto thee; but if not, it shall not be so.* What Elijah was indirectly teaching Elisha here is the importance of "focus". Elijah said it is a hard thing that you have asked; he told Elisha, what you have asked me is almost impossible. But because there is nothing impossible with God, you will get it if only "you can pay the enormous price". Elisha probably will wonder; what price am I going to pay? Is he going to ask me to build a house for God? Or will he ask me to sell everything I have and bring the money to him? Or will he ask me to sacrifice, thousands of cattle for God? Elijah softly said to him, the great price is this; "if you can see me when I am taking from thee you will certainly get what you have asked". Elisha quickly retorted, "What do you mean, I should see you when you are taken, and get a double portion of your spirit"? If it is only to see you and get the double portion of your spirit; that is a small thing for me to do! Elijah responded with a giggle "look Elisha, it is not as easy as you think, I don't mean just look only with your eyes! Of course it is an easy thing for you to look at me with your eyes when I am taking. But you have to look at me with more than your physical eyes, you have to be focused, and concentrate on what you want". If you want a double portion, you have to focus and concentrate on the vision till the very last minute without any distraction because the moment you give in to distraction may be the very moment your answer is knocking at your door, and you will miss it! Let your waking taught be on the vision; let every step be the vision, let all you do reflect and orbit the vision. That is absolutely the only way you can receive your answers. Put your whole heart and vigor into that vision, so much that you will be expended in it. Many people have missed their opportunities to excel because of just one minute distraction; some, because of one week, or one month distraction. The devil is so sneaky that it is exactly when you are closer to realizing your dreams that he brings distractions and you loose focus for just one moment, you were supposed to actualize that your long expected dream.

Caleb is another example for us. His focus was on God's word for the Israelites; that God will bring them into the land flowing with milk and honey. Thus, he saw the giants in the land, as spring board for them to launch. *Num 13:30 And Caleb stilled the people before Moses, and said, Let us go up at once, and possess it; for we are well able to overcome it.* The Lord however appraised and applauded Caleb's focus and undaunted gesture. *Num 14:24 But my servant Caleb, because he had another spirit with him, and **hath followed me fully**, him will I bring into the land whereinto he went; and his seed shall possess it*. That is the power of focus! Caleb followed the Lord's word fully without an iota of distraction. **He followed fully!** Distraction could come from inside you; and it could also come from outside. The distraction from inside you is the most dangerous, because most people won't even see it as distraction. It usually begins as a minute doubt, so minute that you can hardly notice it yourself. You start asking yourself some questions inside you; am I sure I am called to do this? Am I sure this is my talent? Can I do this? Will I not fail? These questions are means to distract you from your course. When next they arise in your heart, discard them without hesitation. If you allow them to sediment in your heart, they will consequently corrode your enthusiasm and detour your focus. The other type of distraction is the one that comes from the outside world. It can come from people, or from one or more activities you are involved in. It can even come from your family; it can also come as a result of you not having adequate finance to do what you intend to do. The only way to overcome distractions is to look unto God who is the giver of the vision; your eyes should never look away from God. Your Focus should steadily be on God. The more you focus on him, the more you get a clear understanding of your vision; and the more you understand your vision, the more you are able to align with it. It is as simple as that! What is needed to get that vision realized therefore is **"focus"**. Focus on God so as to get the grace to focus on your dream. If you can just put in a little more effort to maintain focus on God and on your dream, your story will change for the better. There are a lot of things that will tend to dissuade you from your dreams and cause you to doubt your visions. But be resolute never to give in to doubts and fear. As soon as doubt and fear set into your dreams and visions you are defeated. But if you maintain focus, you will continue to see breakthrough in every challenge; you will get solution to every difficulty; there will be an explanation to every question and there will be water in every dry ground. Events will start connecting in your life like a jigsaw puzzle and your dreams will start getting clearer. Focus is just the key. If you lack focus, you will be no different from Martha; you will be troubled over many things, and will achieve none of them. *Luke 10:41 And Jesus answered and said unto her, Martha, Martha, thou art careful and troubled about many things:* It is where your focus is that you will eventually channel your impetus. If your dream perhaps is to be a great singer, then channel the whole of your enthusiasm without reserve into singing; search for, and seek to break new grounds in the music industry. Be inventive and daring; think of what has not been achieved in the industry, and seek to achieve it, aspire to make a difference. You can do it! Perhaps your own dream is to get to the top in your career, then put in your whole dynamism and resources into that job. Even if people scoff at you because of it, it is not what people think of you that matters, but what you think of yourself. Great men all over the world have at one time or the other in their lives been ridiculed. So don't get dispirited because some folks are making jest of you. Let them keep laughing, but you keep doing what you believe you can do. Put in your whole liveliness into your dream and seek to explore new grounds.

If you do not know what you are made to be, then you will basically have no dream. It is your knowledge of "who you are" and what you can do that sparks up a dream in you. If you fail to know who you are and what you can do, you will emphatically fail to have a dream. If you have no dream; then you will unquestionably have no future; meaning you will eventually be floating and living a life of "maybe and maybe not". This will never lead you any where. You will be living a hopeless life! This is the reason why a lot of people pray and pray for God to give them breakthrough, but it seems far from them. God does not just give breakthrough to somebody jumping from pillar to post, and wandering aimlessly. If you want break through in life, you need to have a dream and a focus. Discover yourself today and get a dream for yourself; then put in concentration into your dream.

**Confidence:** After focus, what you need next is confidence. Confidence is to have a firm trust in somebody to do what he is supposed to do or what he promised to do. It is also to have a strong and firm believe in oneself and abilities. You need a cooperative confidence in other to excel in whatever you do. Firstly, you need confidence in God to fulfill your destiny for you, and bring you into its full actualization, and secondly you need to have an undaunted confidence in yourself. God is the author of every good dream *(James 1:17 Every good gift and every perfect gift is from above, and cometh down from the Father of lights)*. Even those dreams and plans you are yet to think of, it is God that gives it. He puts the vision into your heart, and the seed is sown. Whenever God is mentioned as an author, the next thing that follows is that he is also the finisher. He does not author what he cannot finish. God is writing a book for people to read. That book is you! He will never abandon the book he is writing. He is not like many authors who often run out of ideas and get stuck in the middle of their project. God will never be stuck in the middle of the book he is writing. He has got more than enough ideas to complete it, and make it a sought-after. You are that book which God is writing! You therefore need to put confidence in him to complete the work he has begun in you. The only thing he needs from you is confidence and total trust, and don't worry about how he does it. He is writing the book for his own glory and he will do the marketing of the book all by himself. He has more than enough marketing strategies to market you. You therefore need to abandon yourself into his awesome hand, as an author that will never abandon his write up.

In Rev 22:13; Jesus said of himself, *I am the alpha and omega*. This invariably means he is the beginning, the process, and the end. In *Rev*

*21:6 It is done. I am Alpha and Omega, the beginning and the end. I will give unto him that is athirst of the fountain of the water of life freely.*

This is why your overall confidence must be in God. He began this verse by saying, "it is done, I am alpha and omega" and he concluded the verse by saying, "I will give to him that athirst of the fountain of the water of life freely". Let's see another translation of the Bible, to help us understand this verse better. In the New Living Translation of the Bible, the verse reads *"it is finished; I am alpha and omega, the beginning and the end. To all who are thirsty, I will give the springs of the water of life without charge.* The word "spring" refers to the origin of something; it means a source from which something came in to been. God is therefore saying that from A to Z, he will fulfill your dream and give you satisfaction from the source of life himself which is "himself". However God has promised us not just the happiness you will get in actualizing your dream; but far more than happiness, he has promised to give us contentment and tranquility from the fountain of life. If therefore your satisfaction and success is coming from the very source of life; your life will indisputably be indicative of the limitless life that God has promised us. Your life will know no bounds! Your life will flourish far beyond what you expect. God also called himself as the **"it is done" (Rev 21:6)**. Putting God into your dream means your dream is a done deal; because he is the "it is done to every dream". He gave you the dream; he is the author of the dream, and you need to allow him to be the finisher. He promised you that he will lavish grandeur and brilliance on you, and bring your dreams to fruition. In *Num 23:19 God is not a man, that he should lie; neither the son of man, that he should repent: hath he said, and shall he not do it? or hath he spoken, and shall he not make it good?* More than anything else, you need an undaunted confidence in God, if you ever want to succeed in life. He knows the secret ways, he knows all the short cuts to your destiny and he understands the way in that thick and dangerous path you are threading. He will carry you on his wings and bring you to succor and attainment. *Ex 19:4 Ye have seen what I did unto the Egyptians, and how I bare you on eagles' wings, and brought you unto myself.* This was God talking about how he took the children of Israel through the terrible wilderness they had to go through to get to their promised land. He never failed them in any of his promises to them. He fought for them and carried them on his wings, till he eventually landed them in the land he promised them; which was their dream land. God also is the one that gave you your dream as a promise, and if you will humbly allow him to steer the wheel of your life, he will fight for you, and carry you on his wings. The psalmist said, *Ps 118:8 It is better to trust in the LORD than to put confidence in man.*

## The seed of greatness is in you:

God has deposited the seed of greatness in you; every human being is born with the seed of greatness inside him; *Prov 18:16 A man's **gift maketh** room for him, and **bringeth him** before **great** men.* However, the problem with many folks is that they are oblivious of the fact that the seed of greatness is inside them; and they consequently live their lives in apprehension and inferiority complex. Another problem is that many drift towards the concept that they can never achieve greatness; they see greatness as something meant for only a selected few; and as such it is prohibited for them to attain. But in practicality, God designed man such that every body is a potential candidate for greatness. Many people however do not know how to bring out the greatness from inside them, thus becoming redundant in their drive for greatness. They eventually live and die as mediocre. That is why it is said that the cemetery is the richest place on earth because there are a lot of seeds that never germinated and died along with the people in there. Seeds of powerful inventions, seeds of prolific writers, seeds of articulate speakers, are all in the cemetery.

If a man acknowledges the one who puts the seed inside him; the owner of the seed will eventually show him the way to germinate that seed he has deposited in him. God is the one that has deposited that seed of greatness inside you and he is the only one that can cause the seed to sprout. Above everything else, you have to put confidence and trust in him. Commit your life to him and trust him to make manifest the seed in you and recreate your life.

You are also obligated to have confidence in yourself. One of the mechanisms the devil uses to deter people from manifesting the greatness in them is lack of self confidence. In the opening chapter of this book, it was analyzed that the devil uses three major weapons to restrain people and restrict their growth. Those weapons were seen to be fear, shame and inferiority complex according to Gen 3:10 *And he said, I heard thy voice in the garden, and I was afraid (fear), because I was naked (shame); and I hid myself (inferiority complex).*

Inferiority complex is an unrealistic feeling of general inadequacy caused by actual or supposed inferiority in one sphere, sometimes marked by aggressive behavior in compensation. Lack of confidence in oneself is what begets inferiority complex. Lack of confidence in one's self is the beginning while inferiority complex is the full blown malady of low self esteem. Either the boy (lack of confidence) or man (inferiority complex) is very dangerous and wield devastating results; they limit you and make you sterile; and eventually kill your dream. Lack of confidence is when you don't believe you can do what you are supposed to do. However, the person that is giving you the task, whether God or man, believes you can do it. You as the person who is commissioned to carry out that task do not believe you can do it and consequently pull back. The task will eventually not be carried out or somebody else will do it; but you will loose the reward and glory. To you as a person that has refused that commission, you will feel you are just being real to yourself by not carrying out the task. But in reality you are a coward. You have succeeded in living like a stranger to yourself by not doing what you are capable of doing. The real you can carry out that task. But you have succeeded in shutting your real self in the dark, thus preventing him from doing what he can do. Let this sink inside you from today that you are equal to every task that comes your way. Don't run away from that task; you can do it. You have all what it takes to do it. Before God gives you a task, he has ascertained that you have what it takes to execute the task.

Paul understood the essence of self confidence, and thus wrote in Phil 4: 13, "*I can do all things through Christ which strengthens me"* In other words, if you can just grasp the reality that Christ is in you and he lives in you to strengthen you. This acknowledgement will propel you to believe in yourself and generate self confidence. You can do it! Don't run from that assignment! Only have confidence in God and in yourself. Remember *"you can do all things, through Christ that strengthens you"*. In *Isa 30:15 For thus saith the Lord GOD, the Holy One of Israel; In returning and rest shall ye be saved; in quietness and in confidence shall be your strength*. I encourage you to have an undaunted confidence in yourself today. It is your poise that propels you to the top. Don't run away from that task! In *2 Tim 1:7 For God hath not given us the spirit of fear; but of power, and of love, and of a sound mind*. God has put inside you, the proficiency to overcome every challenge that comes your way.

**UNDERSTANDING YOUR POTENTIALS:**

Here are some guidelines for you to comprehend your capability and maximize them.

1. One way of identifying your potential is by; **what you see yourself doing easily without stress.** You just find yourself consciously and unconsciously doing it recurrently and you derive great joy in doing it. That is your talent. Put your psyche in it and incite originality. The seed is already in you and it will certainly sprout and bring forth greatness if you hold on to it. Maybe it is singing or acting or writing that you do so easily, or whatever it is that you do easily, I counsel you to release that gift from within you and let it blossom. It is the seed of greatness that God has put inside you.

2.  Another way of identifying your talent is by **identifying what you love to do**, but you just feel or think you can't do it. You always admire it when people do it, and wish you could. You always think; oh! I wish I could just do this thing! Then I will be very happy with myself. The fact that you love to do it and wish you can do it is a signal that you probably have the enablement to do it. From all indications, you may not even look like you can do it, but if you try it over and over again without quitting you will see yourself doing it elegantly. One major reason why people are unable to utilize their talent is because they habitually quit early in the venture, after experiencing a temporary defeat. You failed in doing something the first and second time does not mean you don't have the ability to do it. Your initial failure depicts that you have not

yet perfected and mastered that flair. One will always make some little mistakes at the early stage of utilizing your talents, because that talent has been lying dormant in you all your life. Don't just expect that talent to start performing flawlessly all of a sudden. You need some time and patience to get it up and get it flowing. It is just like gold; gold does not glitter all of a sudden. It has to go through a series of process; it must first be purified, and tried before it starts to glint. So also is the talent in you! It must pass through the fire before it glitters. That is why you may initially experience some failures, but don't quit early! Try it again and again.

3. **What is your dream?** What do you actually want to be? Search your heart and see what you feel you can do, even though you are not

perfect in it yet. What is the picture you see of yourself? If your dream is to be a medical doctor, or an inventor, or a singer or writer; then that is the image you have of yourself and you can actually become it! A dream comes from inside you; it buds from within the vast resource of endowment in you. Therefore a dream does not just come if the means and potential to achieve it are not there.  It is the seed in you that propels the dream. If you can dream it, then you can be it because the seed to become it is already in you! Joseph had a dream when he was still very tender. His dream was that he will become so prominent that the sun, moon and eleven stars will pay obeisance to him. His dream was that he will be so significant that nations will honor and respect him. The seed to actualize this dream has already been deposited inside him by God. By his keeping track with God, and maintaining uninterrupted focus in God he actualized the dream. Despite the great hurdles and temptations Joseph went through; that dream came to pass, and nations came and did pay obeisance to him. *Gen 37:9 And he dreamed yet another dream, and told it his brethren, and said, Behold, I have dreamed a dream more; and, behold, the sun and the moon and the eleven stars made obeisance to me...Gen 41:41 And Pharaoh said unto Joseph, See, I have set thee over all the land of Egypt*. Don't allow that dream inside you to die! You already have the seed and potentials to become that great person you dreamt to be. Just keep track with God and maintain focus.

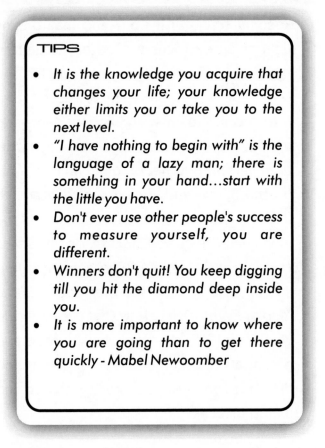

**TIPS**

- It is the knowledge you acquire that changes your life; your knowledge either limits you or take you to the next level.
- "I have nothing to begin with" is the language of a lazy man; there is something in your hand...start with the little you have.
- Don't ever use other people's success to measure yourself, you are different.
- Winners don't quit! You keep digging till you hit the diamond deep inside you.
- It is more important to know where you are going than to get there quickly - Mabel Newoomber

*A man's gift maketh room for him, and bringeth him before great men. - Prov 18:16*

# Enhance Yourself

# ENHANCE YOURSELF

The knowledge you have of yourself could either enrich or deplete your temperament. You cannot live above your knowledge; thus it is imperative for you to seek to know yourself by all means. Know what stuff you are made of, know your strength and weaknesses, know what seed reside within you and get oriented with how you can propagate that precious seed of greatness to get the best from it. Let's take a diagnosis of the process of seed growth, for you to get a better understanding of how to nurture your own seed of greatness.

148

## NATURE OF SEEDS

**In seeds:** before a biological seed can germinate, there is usually a period of dormancy called **<u>seed dormancy</u>**. It is usually a period of rest for the seed after it falls off from the parent plant. Seeds don't just fall off their mother plant today and germinate today. They must undergo a rest period called the dormancy period. This period may be very short or they may be long depending on the nature of the seed. Among the members of the Orchid family, the seeds complete their maturation during this resting period. While in some other plants, chemical changes take place during the period and prepare the seed for germination. Some other seeds have extremely tough seed coats that must soften or decay before water and oxygen can take effect on the seed, to induce the growth of the embryo or before the growing embryo is able to spurt through the seed coat. This is exactly the same thing that takes place in that seed lying deep in you. God created for all seeds to operate and grow in this same way; whether it is spiritual seed or physical seed, it must pass through this same process to grow. The seed inside you also has a dormancy period. A great man does not just turn great overnight! A man does not just discover his abilities the exact day he was born; even though those abilities are innate in him. You don't just discover that you can sing or write or teach or play ball the day you were born. It takes process and time to discover your seed. Between the period you were born into the world and the period you discover your talent is called your dormancy period. It is in this period that God usually prepares and reveals that seed inside you to you, so you groom it. If you fail to discover your seed, you will end up living an aimless life. Your seed will remain dormant in you for the rest of your life, and will never sprout nor profit. This is why a lot of people die with their seeds of greatness without germinating it. They failed to discover their seed in the seed dormancy period. Plant growers can shorten the period of their seed dormancy by soaking the seed in water or in chemical as sulfuric acid, or by heating to crack the seed coat. All this will enable water and oxygen to quickly and easily penetrate the seed coat and effect germination on time. You can also shorten the period of your seed dormancy. But the only way you can do it is to discover your seed on time by means of thorough research on yourself and by fervent prayers. The earlier you discover that seed in you, the shorter your period of seed dormancy, and the longer it takes for you to discover your seed, the longer the period of your seed dormancy.

After a seed has undergone the period of rest (dormancy), the next thing is **germination.**

Germination is thus the resumption of the growth of the seed embryo after the period of dormancy. Germination does not take place unless the seed has been transported to a favorable environment by one of the agent of seed dispersal. The primary conditions needed for a favorable environment for seed germination are <u>water, oxygen and a suitable temperature</u>. Let's now correlate this to the seed inside you. On resumption from your dormancy period, you need a favorable environment with which you can develop your seed. The favorable environments you need are: the quantity of the word of God you take in, the people you move with as close friends and those around you, the effort you put into yourself to groom that seed in you.

1.  **The quantity of the word of God you take in:** The word of God is comparable to the

oxygen that grows your seed. Just like a natural seed cannot sprout without oxygen, so also is the seed in you. It is the word of God that gives life to your seed as a child of God. (*Isa 44:3 For I will pour water upon him that is thirsty, and floods upon the dry ground: I will pour my spirit upon thy seed, and my blessing upon thine offspring*). God is the owner and giver of the seed; therefore it is only by his word that you can stimulate the seed in you to bud and empower it to maturity. If you lack the word of God in you, your talent will be devoid of the potency to bud and mature appropriately; even if it does sprout, it will be maneuvered into the wrong use. The devil will take advantage to manipulate your frail heart into utilizing your flair in the wrong way and eventually miss the essence of that endowment.

2.  **The people you move with as close friends:** Just as the word of God is liken to the oxygen that activates the growth of the seed; the folks around you are liken to the temperature that a natural seed needs to germinate.

Your close friends can contribute immensely to the development of your ability and they can also contribute immensely to the obliteration thereof. You may be thinking how? When your close friends and associates continually mock you and laugh at you over what you are doing or planning to do, you gradually loose interest in it and get discouraged; ultimately you end up in frustration and abandonment of your potential. On the contrary, if the people around you continue to compliment you and encourage you over what you are doing and planning to do, you quickly spring up with the impetus to put your proficiency to work. If you already believe in yourself, you will be encouraged more because of their believing in you. By this you see that your close friends and associates have served as a temperature to regulate the development of your potentiality.

Watch your friends and watch the people around you. If they are the type that always tell you negative and discouraging words about yourself. Then judiciously avoid them and avoid hanging around them. Let's take Samson as a case study in this regard; the seed of greatness in him was destroyed by the person he loved most (Delilah). *Judge 16:4,6,16,17-19 And it came to pass afterward, that he loved a woman in the valley of Sorek, whose name was Delilah... And Delilah said to Samson, Tell me, I pray thee, wherein thy great strength lieth, and wherewith thou mightest be bound to afflict thee... and it came to pass, when she pressed him daily with her words, and urged him, so that his soul was vexed unto death That he told her all his heart, ...And when Delilah saw that he had told her all his heart, she sent and called for the lords of the Philistines, saying, Come up this once, for he hath shewed me all his heart. Then the lords of the Philistines came up unto her, and brought money in their hand. And she made him sleep upon her knees; and she called for a man, and she caused him to shave off the seven locks of his head; and she began to afflict him, and his strength went from him.* If Samson had been cautious enough, he would have discern beforehand what Delilah was up to; and he would have grasp the fact that Delilah was not a good temperature to favor his endowment. Samson was however carried away by sentiments and infatuation and ultimately landed himself in a wrong temperature which eventually lead to the lost of both his seed and his life.

Don't allow sentiments to tie you down to that person that is doing harm to your seed. If you allow sentiments to override your decisions and choice, your seed will be dead before you realize it. Watch the people you move with; they can make you and they can mar you. They are the temperature that regulates the growth of that precious seed of greatness in you.

3.  **The effort you put into yourself to groom that seed:** This is the third environment you need to nurture your ability. It is likened to the water that a natural seed needs to activate the enzymes that instigate germination and growth. You need to water your God given ability day and night, by putting in personal effort to make it grow. The next question therefore is how do you do this?

    A)    Get close to people that have similar gifts; and have done marvelous

157

things with their gifts. Get close to such and learn from their ups and downs. If you are not opportune to physically get close to them, then put in every effort to read about them or ask people about them. This will put you on the guard as to what you should also expect.

B)    Don't sit down idle, waiting for a convenient time to begin. Start doing something with your gift no matter how small it seems to be. If you know you can sing, or write or act or whatever you know you can do, then start doing it. There is no other convenient time to start it than now. Start writing songs and singing; start writing books; if your own talent is to act, then start acting! You can begin in the church acting group. Don't be afraid of failing, because you will not fail. You may make a couple of mistakes at the beginning. However those mistakes are there as springboard to launch you to fulfillment.

C) Encourage yourself daily and see yourself excel in that gift. No other person can encourage you the way you can encourage yourself. The encouragement and encouraging words you speak to yourself is worth more than ten thousand from another person. Encourage yourself about your gift, and make up your mind never to quit.

D) Pray for the growth of your seed (gift) and speak prophetic words over your life.

**The seed of greatness is lying inside you; bring it out today!**

## TIPS

- *If you lack the word of God in you; your talent will be devoid of the potency to mature appropriately.*

- *If you allow sentiments to override your decisions, your seed of greatness will be dead before you realize it.*

- *It is good to dream, but it is better to dream and work. Faith is mighty, but action with faith is mightier. – Thomas Robert Gaines.*

- *He who reigns within himself and rules his passions, desires, and fears is more than a king – John Milton*

- *Encourage yourself daily, no other person can encourage you the way you can encourage yourself.*

*For I will pour water upon him that is thirsty, and floods upon the dry ground: I will pour my spirit upon thy seed, and my blessing upon thine offspring - Isa 44:3*

# 5

# Men of Honour

# MEN OF HONOUR

**H**istory is laden with awesome stories of men who have achieved great feats for their country and for the human race. Some of these men are men that wrestled with one predicament or the other in their life time, but did not allow their dilemma to deter them from their vision. Greatness usually starts with a passion and a vision; you cannot operate in realms of great minds if your vision is myopic and parochial. Your impaired vision will consequently impede the reach of your mind. Stir up to sharpen your vision and broaden your mind, for as far as your eyes can see and your mind can conceive, your hand will reach.

Greatness and success is not automatic, neither can it be staged by principles; it cannot be produced by the application of any formula. It is rather the product of your vision and your mindset. Giving precision and intensity to your vision will ultimately originate greatness. Achievers are men with extra ordinary vision, men that sees solution where others see failure and difficulty; men that sees water in the desert and a road in the Red sea. Nobody was born great, great men are mean men that made themselves great by their feats.

They are men that went the extra mile to make an indelible imprint on the sand of time. You too can be great, if only you can pay the price.

Here are just a handful of the men of honor of our time:

## IDAHOSA, BENSON ANDREW
## 1938 to 1998

Benson Andrew Idahosa was born in Benin City on September 11, 1938 of A poor pagan parents. He was a sickly infant who was always fainting. As a result of his constant illness his father ordered the mother to throw him in the dust bin. When he was eighteen months old he was left on a rubbish heap to die. He was rejected by his father, sent to work on a farm as a servant and was denied education until he was fourteen years old. His education was irregular due to the poor financial status of his parents. He later took correspondence courses from Britain and the United States while working in Bata Shoe Company.

Benson Idahosa, became the archbishop and founder of Church of God Mission International Incorporated with its headquarters in Benin

City, Nigeria, established over 6,000 churches throughout Nigeria and Ghana before 1971. Many of the ministers he supervised pastored churches of 1,000 to 4,000 people. In addition to filling the position of archbishop of Church of God Mission, he was also president of All Nations for Christ Bible Institute, president of Idahosa World Outreach and president of Faith Medical Centre. He held positions in numerous organizations including the college of bishops of the international communion of Christian churches and the Oral Roberts University in Oklahoma.He is also the founder of Benson Idahosa University,Benin city, Nigeria.

## PHILIP EMEAGWALI - SCIENTIST, BORN 1954

A winner of the Gordon Bell prize in 1989, the Nigerian-born computer scientist and geologist is a symbol of African achievement. Emeagwali, voted the 35th greatest African of all time in The New African, played a great role in the birth of the internet.

## MARCUS GARVEY - CIVIL RIGHTS ACTIVIST, 1887-1940

Black nationalist leader, who created a "Back to Africa" movement in the United States. Garvey became an inspiration for future civil rights activists by travelling across America urging African-Americans to be proud of their heritage and to return to the continent. He founded the Black Star Shipping Line and United Negro Improvement Association

## GEORGE WASHINGTON CARVER - BOTANIST, 1864-1943

Dubbed a " black Leonardo" by Time magazine, Carver – born into slavery himself. He is an American scientist and educator, noted especially for his research on the peanut. Carver was internationally recognized for his research in agricultural sciences, and he is credited with having revolutionized agriculture in the Southern United States. As a teacher and as the head of agricultural research at Tuskegee Normal and Industrial Institute (now known as Tuskegee University) in Alabama, Carver dedicated his career to finding uses for plant products and to teaching farmers the advantages of diversifying their crops.

## Kofi Annan - Diplomat,
## Born 1938

Annan was the seventh Secretary-General of the United Nations. He played a great role in working for global peace and was recognized . He also helped to reform the UN and strengthen its peacekeeping abilities.

As secretary general, Annan reorganized the management of the UN in order to increase efficiency and reduce costs, and he improved the organization's relationship with the United States. He rededicated the UN to its traditional goals of economic development, social justice, and international peace. He placed particular importance on combating the epidemic of acquired immunodeficiency syndrome (AIDS) and improving human rights worldwide. In his farewell address as secretary general, Annan emphasized the importance of human rights, saying, "Human rights and the rule of law are vital to global security and prosperity."

## MARTIN LUTHER KING - CIVIL RIGHTS ACTIVIST,
## 1929-68

The figurehead of the American Civil Rights Movement. He is known for leading the civil rights movement in the United States and Advocating nonviolent protest against segregation and racial discrimination.

After his assassination in 1968, King became a symbol of protest in the struggle for racial justice.

## MIRIAM MAKEBA - MUSICIAN, ACTIVIST,
## Born 1932

Known as " Mama Africa", one of the first musicians to bring African music to the rest of the world. She was exiled by the South African government in 1960 after speaking out against apartheid in an address at the United Nations. A political exile from 1960 to 1990, Makeba was a strong vocal opponent of the South African racial segregation policy of apartheid, and her records were banned in South Africa

## NELSON MANDELA - POLITICAL ACTIVIST,
## Born 1918

A key anti-apartheid figure in South Africa, Mandela spent 27 years in prison for the cause. After his release, he became the country's first fully democratically elected president and leader of the African National Congress.

## BOB MARLEY - MUSICIAN,
## 1945-81

Jamaican singer, guitarist, and songwriter, a pioneer of reggae music. Considered one of the greatest artists of the genre, he was the first reggae performer to achieve significant international stardom.

Bob Marley brought reggae to a worldwide audience, and is a hero in Jamaica as well as being seen by many Rastafarians as a prophet. His albums and shows with his band, The Wailers, were legendary.

## Rosa Parks - Activist, 1913-2005

African American civil rights activist. In 1955 in Montgomery, Alabama, Parks refused to give up her bus seat to a white man. Her action led to the Montgomery bus boycott, an organized, citywide protest against segregation that used nonviolent tactics. Parks's refusal to give up her seat on an Alabama bus became a symbolic moment in the American civil rights movement. The fallout launched Martin Luther King Jr to fame. The incident sparked a mass boycott of the transport system by the Black community. Rosa Parks's personal act of defiance opened a decisive chapter in the civil rights movement in the United States.

## Wole Soyinka - Poet, writer, playwright, born 1934

Nigerian playwright, poet, novelist, and lecturer, whose writings draw on African tradition and mythology while employing Western literary forms. In 1986 Soyinka became the first African writer and the first black writer to win the Nobel Prize in literature. One of the leading writers in Africa, Soyinka won the Nobel Prize for Literature in 1986.

His work often concentrates on oppression and tyranny. He has also played a huge role in Nigerian politics and was imprisoned in 1967 during the country's civil war

## Archbishop Desmond Tutu - Cleric, campaigner, born 1931

A key figure in the overthrow of apartheid in South Africa, Tutu was chosen by President Mandela to chair the Truth and Reconciliation Commission. In 1975 he became the first black Anglican Dean of Johannesburg, and was awarded the Nobel Peace Prize in 1985.

Oprah Winfrey - Media tycoon, born 1954 A living American institution, she is seen by some as the most influential woman in the world. At the centre of her various projects is her TV chat show which is syndicated around the world. In 2006 Winfrey became the world's first black woman billionaire.

## Malcolm X - Civil rights activist, 1925-65

Malcolm X was a major campaigner for black power and opposed the idea of racial equality.

He is Known For Advocating black nationalism and promoting black self-respect and economic self-help A believer in militant protest, he was assassinated not long after leaving the Nation of Islam and creating the Organization of Afro-American Unity.

## Muhammad Ali - Boxer, born 1942

Widely considered to be the greatest athlete of all time. one of the greatest fighters in the history of the sport. Colorful, talented, and sometimes controversial, Ali entertained fans and intimidated opponents. His boxing style involved graceful footwork and powerful jabs. He also became famous for bragging about himself, often in his own verse. Ali once described his skills by saying that he could "float like a butterfly, sting like a bee." In 1978 he became the first boxer to win the world heavyweight championship title three different times.   He was also a key figure in the civil-rights movement after refusing to fight in Vietnam because of how blacks were treated in America.

## Lewis Howard Latimer - Inventor, 1848-1928

The son of escaped slaves, Latimer is considered one of the greatest black inventors, notably due to his improvement of carbon filaments in light bulbs. He worked with Thomas Edison and Alexander Bell and secured many different patents

## Bill Gates

Bill Gates, born in 1955, American business executive, who serves as chairman of Microsoft Corporation, the leading computer software company in the United States. Gates cofounded Microsoft in 1975 with high school friend Paul Allen. The company's success made Gates one of the most influential figures in the computer industry and, eventually, one of the richest people in the world.

## STEVE JOBS

February 24, 1955 – October 5, 2011) was an American businessman and inventor widely recognized as a charismatic pioneer of the <u>personal computer revolution</u>. He was co-founder, chairman, and chief executive officer of <u>Apple Inc</u>

In the late 1970s, Apple co-founder <u>Steve Wozniak</u> engineered one of the first commercially successful lines of personal computers, the <u>Apple II series</u>. Jobs directed its aesthetic design and marketing along with <u>A.C. "Mike" Markkula, Jr.</u> and others.

In the early 1980s, Jobs was among the first to see the commercial potential of Xerox PARC's mouse-driven graphical user interface, which led to the creation of the <u>Apple Lisa</u> (engineered by Ken Rothmuller and John Couch) and, one year later, creation of Apple employee Jef Raskin's Macintosh. After losing a power struggle with the board of directors in 1985, Jobs left Apple and founded NeXT, a computer platform development company specializing in the higher-education and business markets.

In 1986, he acquired the computer graphics division of Lucasfilm Ltd, which was spun off as Pixar Animation Studios.[8] He was credited in *Toy Story* (1995) as an executive producer. He remained CEO and majority shareholder at 50.1 percent until its acquisition by The Walt Disney Company in 2006. Making Jobs Disney's largest individual shareholder at seven percent and a member of Disney's Board of Directors.

In 1996, NeXT was acquired by Apple. The deal brought Jobs back to the company he co-founded, and provided Apple with the NeXTSTEP codebase, from which the Mac OS X was developed."[12] Jobs was named Apple advisor in 1996, interim CEO in 1997, and CEO from 2000 until his resignation.

(Extracted from wikipedia)

## BARACK HUSSEIN OBAMA II

(born August 4, 1961) is the 44th and current President of the United States. He is the first African American to hold the office. Obama previously served as a United States Senator from Illinois, from January 2005 until he resigned following his victory in the 2008 presidential election.

Born in Honolulu, Hawaii, Obama is a graduate of Columbia University and Harvard Law School, where he was the president of the *Harvard Law Review*. He was a community organizer in Chicago before earning his law degree. He worked as a civil rights attorney in Chicago and taught constitutional law at the

University of Chicago Law School from 1992 to 2004. He served three terms representing the 13th District in the Illinois Senate from 1997 to 2004.

Following an unsuccessful bid against the Democratic incumbent for a seat in the United States House of Representatives in 2000, Obama ran for the United States Senate in 2004. Several events brought him to national attention during the campaign, including his victory in the March 2004 Illinois Democratic primary for the Senate election and his keynote address at the Democratic National Convention in July 2004. He won election to the U.S. Senate in Illinois in November 2004.

His presidential campaign began in February 2007, and after a close campaign in the 2008 Democratic Party presidential primaries against Hillary Rodham Clinton, he won his party's nomination. In the 2008 presidential election, he defeated Republican nominee John McCain, and was inaugurated as president on January 20, 2009. In October 2009, Obama was named the 2009 Nobel Peace Prize laureate. (Extracted from wikipedia)

## ALEXANDER GRAHAM BELL

In 1876, at the age of 29, Alexander Graham Bell invented his telephone. In 1877, he formed the Bell Telephone Company. Alexander Graham Bell might easily have been content with the success of his telephone invention. His many laboratory notebooks demonstrate, however, that he was driven by a genuine and rare intellectual curiosity that kept him regularly searching, striving, and wanting always to learn and to create. He would continue to test out new ideas through a long and productive life. He would explore the realm of communications as well as engage in a great variety of scientific activities involving kites, airplanes, tetrahedral structures, sheep-breeding, artificial respiration, desalinization and water distillation, and hydrofoils.